The
CHEW

The CHEW

FOOD. LIFE. FUN.

Edited by Peter Kaminsky and Ashley Archer

HYPERION

new york

Photo Credits

Craig Sjodin/ABC: headshots and pp. ii, 124, 170; Donna Svennevik/ABC: pp. 7, 10, 12, 14, 23, 30, 66, 67, 71, 78, 92, 98, 104, 118, 127, 135, 141, 161, 168, 169, 184, 197, 199, 201, 213; Fred Lee/ ABC: p. 176; Heidi Gutman/ABC: pp. 17, 110, 111, 113, 139, 145; Ida Mae Astute/ABC: pp. 68, 69, 77, 107, 125, 180, 193, 215; Jeff Neira/ABC: pp. 115, 117, 163; Lorenzo Bevilaqua/ABC: pp. 3, 33, 55, 57, 58, 73, 86, 115, 126, 214; Lou Rocco/ABC: pp. vi, 11, 12, 77, 91, 205, 216, 221

Food photography by Andrew Scrivani

Food styling by Martha Tinkler, Jackie Rothong, and Kevin Mendlin

Prop styling by Francine Degni

Book design by Vertigo Design NYC

Copyright © 2012 Hyperion/ABC

Library of Congress Cataloging-in-Publication Data

The Chew : food, life, fun / The Chew. — 1st ed.
   p. cm.
  ISBN 978-1-4013-1106-3 (pbk.)
1. Cooking. 2. Chew (Television program) 3. Celebrity chefs—United States—Interviews. I. Chew (Television program) II. Title.
  TX714C46668 2012
  641.3—dc23

                2012018523

Hyperion books are available for special promotions and premiums. For details contact the HarperCollins Special Markets Department in the New York office at 212-207-7528, fax 212-207-7222, or email spsales@harpercollins.com.

FIRST EDITION

10   9   8   7   6   5   4   3   2   1

Extreme superspecial thanks to
Kerry McConnell, without whom
this book would have been
impossible and much less fun

CONTENTS

Introduction by Gordon Elliott,
Executive Producer   2

FALL   8

WINTER   64

SPRING   122

SUMMER   166

Acknowledgments   224

The Chew List of Recipes   225

Index   227

The
CHEW

Introduction

By Gordon Elliott, EXECUTIVE PRODUCER

The CHEW was created in about 20 minutes, like a fully formed song just waiting to be written by a hungover rock star. Brian Frons, then head of ABC daytime, a lovely man, was chatting with me one day and threw out the question, "What would you do with an hour on ABC daytime?"

Being a cable TV producer, it was rare anyone asked my opinion of anything. I had one shot and nothing to lose, so I began a stream of consciousness ramble that had been running around my head for years.

I had always imagined a group of friends with lifestyle skills, wit, and real camaraderie that could show viewers how to get a little more out of their daily routines. Not fancy stuff, not expensive, just how to get through the day with a better meal, a smarter choice, a useful tip, a few laughs. If it was done right, I hoped it would feel like a party in the kitchen. TV that made you feel the time you spent watching wasn't wasted.

Brian paused. I imagined I'd bored him rigid by this point.

"What would you call it?"

The name was pure cheek.

"Well, it's a mix of food and a group host format like *The View*, so *The Chew* seems blindly obvious."

I figured he thought I was just kidding around. Neither of us was. *The Chew* was born.

I immediately sat down with the very smart Mark Schneider, my managing director and trusted consigliere. Our usual easy collaboration made it all look doable. Without him it would have been a nightmare. I took a deep breath and made a casting note to myself. I imagined a group of friends effortlessly preparing dinner, splashing Chardonnay and laughter with each other. I wrote the type of "characters" they would be—like a scene from *The Big Chill*.

The host of the party—generous, witty, and well rounded.

The funny guy with a cheeky point of view but also something solid to him.

The curious younger woman with a mix of humility and smarts.

The "mother love" figure with life under her belt but still laughs easily.

The older guy with wisdom and skill—the father figure.

Things began to come together quickly. Randy Barone, the show's eventual godfather at ABC, rushed into my office the first week of casting with a tape of Daphne Oz. She had just made her first-ever appearance on her father's TV program, *The Dr. Oz Show*. Her poise, humor, and humility were obvious. We had coffee. She wasn't looking to be on TV; she wanted to study and write. She was not overeager, like a presidential nominee who doesn't seem to want the gig. This only made her an even more attractive candidate.

Similar to many women, her relationship with food was complex. She had faced terrible insecurity about her body image growing up and knew that constant dieting only fed the beast—pun intended. Daphne eventually found a daily routine that helped her shed her excess 30 pounds and keep it off permanently. She then wrote a book about her search and solutions. It was a *New York Times* bestseller. Not bad for a twenty-three-year-old.

Daphne was newly married, curious, practical, and looking for balance—in her body, work, food, and career. Add a wicked sense of humor and an ability to give as good as she got and you understand why I called her the following day and offered her the job. One down, four to go.

The easy ones? Michael Symon and Mario Batali, two of the most congenial cooks ever to grace the tube. Mario—like Madonna—needs only a first name to identify him to millions of fans of his television and restaurant empire. Michael's stellar reputation was forged in the fires of *Iron Chef*, and he is the master of a heartland domain of successful and terrific restaurants. Working with them over the years, I knew what cheeky, funny men they were. Stylishly competent, they made cooking in stultifying kitchens eight days a week look sexy. Blunt but charming with hearts the size of holiday hams, they were huge TV stars in their own right. That was the problem. They had great lives and didn't need the money, the extra fame, or the time away from their families.

3

But I knew their weakness. Like all great chefs, they are both congenital pleasers. They live to make people happy. I explained this was their dream show. A chance to tell their stories and cook their food in real time, to hang out together and show folks how fun cooking can be. That and a couple pounds of fifty-dollar bills helped do the trick.

From the first time I saw Carla Hall on *Top Chef*, I could see she didn't cook to impress the judges as much as she grooved on her blend of food, love, and soul and the audience sensed it. Like Michael and Mario, nothing makes her happier than standing next to a new friend and showing them a long-learned recipe. She takes them into her calming, comforting world. I needed that magic on the show. I called, she screamed. I found out later she screams a lot. Her joy is high volume.

Clinton came out of the blue at the last moment. We were a week away from announcing the show and still lacked a master of ceremonies. I was starting to sweat and began checking my list of usual suspects when Randy Barone threw open my door again and walked in with Clinton Kelly, fresh from his appearance on *The View* promoting his relationship with Macy's as the company's spokesman. He walked into the room with a confident grin and a hilarious story, sweeping everyone off their feet and into party mode. I had never seen him on TV before and was staggered by how naturally he fit in. He was a true natural host. He listened carefully and, with the mental suppleness of a Russian gymnast, directed conversation to a graceful point, making people feel funnier than they really were. I was as excited as a fat boy in a bakery. I couldn't wait to bring them all together and see if they liked one another as much as I liked them individually.

They did. And the result, as they say, is in the chocolate volcano pudding: five real friends doing what they love, adding a little smarts and fun into the TV world.

You can't fake this stuff. People can tell. That's why the show is a hit.

Writing this book felt like a natural evolution. *The Chew* was always designed to be useful, but the information our hosts naturally spilled into the show soon became a flood. Beyond just recipes and cooking times, their fertile minds bore a bumper crop of life-enhancing tips that felt like a master class in useful fun. We wanted to keep the unique voice of the show intact, so we literally took the words off the screen, added some beautiful shots of the food, and threw a fellow host's side comment in here and there, just as they do on-air.

We hope we've captured the mood created on-screen and continued that spark to try something different. As Clinton says, "Small changes can make big differences in your life," so go ahead, pick one and try it out. Or just sit there and enjoy a lazy, delicious read.

I hope you enjoy the result.

The Chew icons

 LIGHT AND HEALTHY

 SIMPLE ITALIAN

 VIEWERS' CHOICE

 TWO-FER (Two Meals in One)

 5-IN-5 (5 Ingredients in 5 Minutes)

 KID FRIENDLY

 COCKTAIL

Each recipe includes skill level (Easy or Moderate) and price range ($ for recipes that cost under $5 to make, $$ for recipes that cost under $10, and $$$ for recipes that cost over $10).

Love at First Bite

Clinton

Sometimes one bite is all it takes to fall in love. Here's a little bit about the foods that we ate for the first time that we just fell in love with and couldn't get enough of from then on.

Carla

I was in Milan . . . I was about twenty-six years old . . . and I bit into this slice of pizza that I shared with a friend . . . it was cut with scissors and the crust was perfectly crisp with not so much topping. I remember taking a bite and going, "Oh my god, this is delicious. This is pizza! Yeah!"

Daphne

I was in Barcelona and I had something I called garlic butter-basted shrimp. You sucked them out of the head. It was a totally mind-boggling experience and the most delicious shrimp I've ever had. And I don't know what the recipe is so I can't make them for myself, which is sad.

Michael

My favorite bites of food always happened with family. And it was in the basement of my yiayia's house . . . that's where we ate dinner. She had a kitchen down there and a kitchen upstairs. The dish was her bisticchio: layered baked pasta. Oh god. I mean, I remember biting into it and thinking, "This is what I wanna cook. This is why I wanna be a chef." Food makes everybody so happy.

Mario

I was lucky enough to go to high school in Madrid. My friends and I discovered this little place where they made calamari en su tinta. Sounds complicated, but basically it's fried calamari with garlic and salt and pimento stuffed into a soft bread with a lot of crust on it and then drizzled with an aioli with black squid ink in it. So you eat it and then you look at each other and go, "Is there anything in my teeth?" They looked pretty gross—actually that's probably understating it—but boy, was it good!

Clinton

I was thirteen, with my grandparents in Carmel, California, a beautiful city, and we went to a restaurant called the Clam Box where I had lobster thermidor. It was so fancy. I thought to myself, "When I grow up, I'm gonna be fancy!"

Daphne

And here you are!

Clinton

And here I am!

Daphne

You're freakin' fancy!

Clinton

It was a life-changing moment.
Love at first bite.

7

FALL

ROASTED AUTUMN VEGETABLES, 15 | CHESTNUT CREPES WITH MUSHROOMS AND RADICCHIO SALAD, 16 | EGGS WITH SWEET POTATO APPLE PANCAKES, 18 | MONTE CRISTO SANDWICH, 20 | CHILE CHICKEN FLAUTAS, 21 | EGGPLANT PARMIGIANINO, 24 | STUFFED MUSHROOMS, 25 | SPAGHETTI SQUASH FRITTERS, 27 | WINE-STAINED PASTA WITH SAUSAGE MEATBALLS AND CAULIFLOWER, 29 | GENERAL TSO'S CHICKEN, 31 | ROASTED CHICKEN WITH SWEET POTATOES AND SAGE, 32 | CAST-IRON PORK PIE, 34 | CRISPY LIME AND CILANTRO CHICKEN WINGS, 37 | LEMON SAGE TURKEY, 42 | CHESTNUT MERGUEZ STUFFING, 44 | MUSHROOM AND VEGETABLE STUFFING, 45 | PAN-SEARED TURKEY WITH GREMOLATA, 47 | BRUSSELS SPROUTS À LA "RUSS" WITH WALNUTS AND CAPERS, 48 | CHOCOLATE PUMPKIN PIE, 51 | BATTER FRIED APPLE RINGS, 52 | CHEW CHEW CLUSTERS, 53 | TEN-GALLON APPLE PIE, 54 | BLT BLOODY MARY, 56 | THE STINTON, 59 | POMEGRANATE SUNSET, 61 | CRANBERRY SODA, 62

Clinton

Q: **You are the host of a dinner party where a lot of people gather in the kitchen. What's required to make that happen, and how do you keep the vibe going and involve people?**

Clinton: I'm very conscious of the people who are watching the show, the people in the audience, and the people on camera with me. I try to be as welcoming as possible and nonthreatening and to keep the conversation going. There are certain things you talk about at a dinner party and there are certain things you don't talk about at a dinner party. So just like at a good dinner party, we avoid super confrontational topics and keep to the things that everybody loves: food, and family, what we did on the weekend, etc. There are many places in television where you can find disagreements, arguing, screaming. Not our style.

Q: **What's special about *The Chew*?**

Clinton: We are about more than food. We're also about family and fun, and how the average American lives his or her life. The average person eats three meals a day (maybe even four, according to some statistics I've seen about being overweight). Cooking should be part of everyone's life. So what we are doing on the show is living our lives and cooking at the same time, if that makes sense. We are not just talking about food. I do style segments that feel at home on *The Chew* because you eat every day and you put clothes on your body every day. So yes, there is nothing else like this on television. We have developed a category of our own.

Chew fans gear up for the Super Bowl.

An audience member sings karaoke with an enchanted Clinton Kelly.

Q: **The audience is really a very important cast member. Is that something that has developed over time? How does that feel?**

Clinton: Well, we all love performing in front of an audience. It brings life to a show. There are 150 people who have gotten up in the morning who have decided to come see us do what we do. They give us the best kind of instant feedback. If you land a good joke it feels great, it gives us a jolt of energy. Their reaction is the best guide to help us keep tabs on if we are handling the right thing, the right subjects. You can tell by the live studio audience and their reaction how the audience at home is going to be accepting of a topic. If you see a couple of people's eyes glaze over, then you know you have a million eyes glazing over at home. We are really in touch with our audience more than any other cooking show. So many cooking shows are done in a studio and you have no idea how the people are responding to it. We have a perfect idea of how they are responding because we see them.

Q: **When you invite an audience member on camera, it's like they are stepping into a friend's kitchen. There's such a level of comfort, even though they are probably on TV for the very first time. Is that something you facilitate, or is that the vibe of the show?**

Clinton: I think it's the vibe of the show. I mean, I really believe that the five of us are kind people at heart. That resonates with our audience. We love sharing recipes with people, we love making cocktails with people, we love the idea of coming together. It's not about ego, the show is not about ego—that's really the amazing thing about *The Chew*, where there are five hosts. There are no big egos, and I think that the audience gets that and they want to be a part of that because we're not intimidating.

Q: **All the hosts have had such successful careers. Are there really no egos on the set? Be honest!**

Clinton: You never know when you throw five people together how they're going to interact with each other. But we all got along beautifully from the beginning and it's kind of shocking. You know, what are your chances of putting five people in a room and having them all become great friends? Pretty rare. I can honestly say that we are not competitive with each other. Well, except maybe when it came to our chili competition (see page 92).

Q: **You are the host of the show, but you also cook and you understand food. Who's the real Clinton?**

Clinton: Well, here's the thing about me. I've been on TV now for the better part of a decade. Um, I never wanted to be a TV star. I never wanted to be a television host. I was just doing my thing and I fell into it. I've always wanted to live my life in the most pleasing way to me, and my life is not necessarily my career. My life is what I do when I'm not getting paid. That is the time that I spend with my family, that's the time I spend with my friends. Those are the most important things to me. I will choose my family, my friends, and my dog every day of the week over my career. That's my number one priority. What people have said to me over the past decade is sort of that I make people over and talk about fashion. That's not who I am. That's a part of who I am. That's my job. It's a small part of me as a person. Who I am as a person is a lot more of a homebody, a home cook, and somebody who just enjoys entertaining. So what *The Chew* allows me to do is bring who I really am to television.

Q: **How has this group changed in the year you've been on the air?**

Clinton: The biggest change that has happened is that we are all five friends off-camera. We call each other up, we text each other, we see each other for a drink outside of the show. That has definitely made the show better, the fact that we genuinely like each other and want to spend time with each other. I look forward to coming to work and that's not been the case for me for a long time.

ROASTED AUTUMN VEGETABLES

SERVES 4 | **Skill Level: EASY** | **Cook Time: 30 mins.** | **Prep Time: 20 mins.** | **Cost: $**

This is a recipe that practically goes in one dish and comes out 30 minutes later ready to eat! With a side salad and maybe a baguette, you've got dinner. Lentils are probably the ingredient that I buy the most. I inherit that from the Turkish side of my family. We use lentils in a lot of ways to complement meat dishes but also sometimes as a substitute for meat. For vegetarians, they are a nutrient-dense, protein-dense food with the meaty consistency we all crave.

This medley features carrots and shallots, which develop a savory sweetness, and Brussels sprouts, which are at their pinnacle of flavor in the fall. When I cook for my husband after a day's work, I want to make dishes that are relatively easy and not about a whole big production. This is just that.

4 small carrots, halved lengthwise

3 shallots, halved

1 butternut squash, halved, seeded, and cut into ½-inch slices

½ pound Brussels sprouts, halved

4 cloves garlic

6 tablespoons extra virgin olive oil

Salt

Freshly ground pepper

½ cup dried black lentils, rinsed

½ an onion

1 bay leaf

3 tablespoons apple cider vinegar

1 tablespoon Dijon mustard

½ pound arugula

1. Preheat the oven to 400 °F.

2. In a large bowl, combine the carrots, shallots, squash, Brussels sprouts, and garlic. Drizzle 2 tablespoons of the extra virgin olive oil, and season with salt and pepper. Toss to coat. Pour vegetables onto a sheet tray and roast in the oven for 30 minutes, tossing once, halfway through.

3. Meanwhile, prepare the lentils by putting them into a small saucepan and covering with water by 2 inches. Add the onion and bay leaf. Bring to a boil, then simmer covered for 20 minutes, or until tender. Drain and discard the onion, season with salt and pepper, and set aside.

4. Once the vegetables are finished roasting, remove the garlic. Peel and mash the garlic in a small bowl, combine with the remaining 4 tablespoons of extra virgin olive oil, apple cider vinegar, and Dijon mustard, and whisk into a vinaigrette. Toss the lentils with the vinaigrette, fold in the arugula leaves, and then top with roasted vegetables to serve.

Some advice to new lentil lovers

With lentils, you want to add flavor while they cook. I usually boil them in water with an onion studded with cloves, some bay leaves, and a little olive oil. Then walk away and let the ingredients get to know one another. A low simmer is the way to go. Cook until they are al dente, with just a little tooth resistance. Mushy lentils are no fun. I like to use red lentils for soup because they're already cracked, they're really creamy, and they give a nice starchiness to the soup. I would use green (Puy) lentils for a salad, and I might use brown lentils for a heartier soup or casserole where I want the lentils to hold their shape.

CHESTNUT CREPES WITH MUSHROOMS & RADICCHIO SALAD

SERVES 6 | **Skill Level: MODERATE** | **Cook Time: 30 mins.** | **Prep Time: 15 mins.** | **Cost: $$**

Inactive Prep Time: 20 mins. – 1 hr.

In World War I, when the supply lines were cut, the hill country folk of Emilia-Romagna, Italy, had to make everything with chestnuts, including flour for crepes. So when I opened my restaurant Babbo, I put these crepes on the menu and they have never come off it. Gwyneth Paltrow, who was first my customer and is now my friend, ordered it on her first visit and, according to her, every time since, which is why we chose to make it when Gwyneth visited The Chew. *She once paid me the highest compliment a chef can receive: My crepes always tasted the same. Now you might think a chef wants to hear "Wow! It was so delicious!" But that's not true. If someone orders something more than once, you already know they think it's great. The real thing that moves a chef's heart is to know that you can turn out something good consistently. Quick, easy, delicious, that's enough to get into my recipe Hall of Fame.*

FOR THE CREPE:

½ cup chestnut flour

¼ cup all-purpose flour

2 eggs

1 cup whole milk

Salt

Freshly ground black pepper

4 tablespoons butter, melted

FOR THE FILLING:

4 tablespoons extra virgin olive oil

3 shallots, minced

1 pound mixed mushrooms, thinly sliced

2 sprigs fresh rosemary, minced

2 sprigs thyme (leaves only)

Salt, to taste

Freshly ground black pepper, to taste

TO MAKE THE BATTER:

1. Place the two flours in a mixing bowl. Add the eggs one at a time, whisking to combine. Add the milk bit by bit, and whisk to combine, until all the milk is incorporated. Season with salt and pepper. Allow the batter to stand for 20 minutes to an hour.

TO MAKE THE FILLING:

2. In a small saucepan, heat the oil over medium heat, until smoking. Add the shallots and cook until soft, about 8–10 minutes.

3. Add the mushrooms and cook until softened, about 10 minutes.

4. Add the rosemary and thyme, and stir to combine. Season to taste with salt and pepper. Remove from the heat and set aside.

TO MAKE THE CREPES:

5. Heat a 6-inch nonstick pan over high heat until hot,

We all need a rest

Any batter with flour, eggs, and milk in it always improves if you let it rest. Leaving it overnight gives you a beautiful, smooth, silky batter.

and brush with the butter. Turn the heat down to medium and pour 1½ tablespoons of batter into the pan. Cook until pale golden on the bottom, about 1 minute. Flip and cook just 5–10 seconds on the second side. Remove and set aside. Continue the process until all the batter has been used. At this point you can freeze the crepes. Wrap crepes tightly in plastic and freeze.

FOR THE SALAD:

3 tablespoons extra virgin olive oil

3 tablespoons good balsamic vinegar

1 head radicchio lettuce, shredded

¼ cup freshly grated Parmigiano-Reggiano, to serve

TO ASSEMBLE:

6. Preheat the oven to 350 °F.

7. Use 2 tablespoons of the melted butter to coat the bottom and sides of a 10-by-8-inch ceramic baking dish. Fill each crepe with some of the mushroom mixture and fold. Put the filled crepes into the buttered dish and drizzle top with remaining butter. Put into the oven for about 15 minutes.

8. In the meantime, make a vinaigrette by slowly adding the olive oil to the balsamic vinegar, whisking to emulsify. Use the vinaigrette to dress the radicchio.

9. When the crepes are hot, remove from the oven and divide evenly among heated plates. Top the crepes with the radicchio salad and sprinkle with the grated Parmigiano-Reggiano. Drizzle with balsamic vinegar to taste and serve warm.

Mario chats with his friend Gwyneth as she takes over the stove.

EGGS WITH SWEET POTATO APPLE PANCAKES

| SERVES 5 | Skill Level: EASY | Cook Time: 20 mins. | Prep Time: 10 mins. | Cost: $ |

Simple, delicious, healthy, and affordable: that's my definition of a recipe worth learning. These sweet potato and apple pancakes are a good way to get your kids to eat whole, unprocessed ingredients by appealing to a child's natural sweet tooth. Come to think of it, they appeal to my grown-up sweet tooth too. The basting technique with the eggs produces a beautiful sunny-side up, with very little butter or oil required. In a time when some people say that using whole, un-processed ingredients is more expensive than fast food (not true), it's refreshing to find a meal for under two dollars that is made only with whole ingredients, including a fruit and a vegetable.

5 fresh eggs

⅓ cup olive oil, plus more if needed

1 sweet potato, peeled and grated

½ onion, peeled and grated

½ apple, peeled and grated

1 carrot, peeled and grated

2 egg whites, lightly beaten

¼ cup all-purpose flour

½ teaspoon salt

½ teaspoon pepper

TO MAKE THE EGGS:

1. Heat a large nonstick skillet over medium heat and brush or spray with olive oil. Add the eggs in batches and cook until the whites just begin to change color, about 2 minutes. Add a splash of water and steam until the whites have set but the yolk is still runny. Serve with the pancakes.

TO MAKE THE SWEET POTATO PANCAKES:

2. In a medium-sized skillet, heat ⅓ cup olive oil to medi-um-high heat.

3. Grate the sweet potato, onion, apple, and carrot. Wring out the liquid in a cheesecloth or paper towel (this is to en-sure the pancakes won't be soggy). Then, in a large bowl, place the grated ingredients, egg whites, and flour. Add the salt and pepper. Mix well.

4. Drop enough batter into the hot oil to make 2½- to 3-inch pancakes. Add more oil, as needed, and fry cakes in batches, until golden on each side.

5. To serve, place 2 pancakes on a plate and top with a basted egg.

Wring, wring

My trick for crispy pancakes is to wrap my grated sweet potatoes and apples in cheesecloth and then wring them out by tightening the cloth. Extra added bonus: all that juice is delicious and healthful.

Steamed and stupendous

As soon as the egg whites begin to set, add a tiny bit of water to the pan and cover it. The steam will cook the eggs and leave you with a yummy runny yolk. Very little butter or oil needed.

MONTE CRISTO SANDWICH

SERVES 4 | Skill Level: EASY | Cook Time: 15 mins. | Prep Time: 20 mins. | Cost: $

First invented in the 1970s, this is the granddaddy of the gourmet grilled sandwich craze. For sure the Count of Monte Cristo never ate such a sandwich. In fact, I have heard that it was born in Disney World at a concession next to the Pirates of the Caribbean . . . but, hey, we know from watching Johnny Depp as Captain Jack Sparrow that his meals were pretty much confined to the rum food group.

After you batter the sandwich, you fry it in a skillet. To serve, I hit it with a good gob of jam, spank it with powdered sugar, garnish with a couple of jalapeños, and add a fried egg on the side. It looked so good that I swear when we took a close-up, Clinton was tempted to eat the monitor.

FOR THE MONTE CRISTO:

Vegetable oil, for frying

1 egg, lightly beaten

¾ cup milk

¾ cup flour

2 teaspoons baking powder

Salt

Pepper

4 tablespoons mustard

8 slices thick-cut white bread

4 slices Fontina cheese

4 slices ham

4 slices smoked turkey

¼ cup pickled jalapeños (optional)

Powdered sugar, for garnish

Jam (optional)

FOR THE FRIED EGGS:

1 tablespoon butter

4 eggs

1. Preheat 2 inches vegetable oil to 360 °F in a large cast-iron skillet.

2. In a shallow baking dish, whisk together the egg and milk. Stir in the flour and baking powder, and season with salt and pepper.

3. Spread mustard on the bread slices. Sandwich each piece of Fontina cheese between one slice of ham and one slice of turkey. Add a couple of pickled jalapeños, if desired, and then sandwich between two pieces of bread.

4. Coat the sandwiches evenly on all sides with the batter. Drop into the oil, and fry until golden brown and crisp. Remove to a paper towel–lined plate, and sprinkle with powdered sugar and add a spoonful of your favorite jam, if desired.

5. For the eggs, heat the butter in a nonstick skillet over medium heat. Once the butter has foamed and subsided, crack each egg into the skillet and fry until the yolk is set.

6. Serve a fried egg alongside each Monte Cristo.

CHILE CHICKEN FLAUTAS

| SERVES 6 | Skill Level: EASY | Cook Time: 1 hr. | Prep Time: 15 mins. | Cost: $ |

In Spanish, flauta means "flute," but I've never seen a flute that looks or sounds like these stuffed fried tortillas. Still, they make beautiful eating music. You can make them from scratch, as we do here, or you can fill them up with just about any leftover, including lasagna. Of course, that may just be the Italian in me speaking: I have yet to find the dish that can't be helped along with a little leftover lasagna. Okay, maybe cupcakes can't, but anything non-sweet is longing for a date with yesterday's lasagna.

As with so much Mexican food, a chile is more than just a chile. There are fresh chilies, dried chilies, smoked chilies, and pickled chilies, and all of them go into these chicken flautas for a beautiful, complex mix of flavors.

Flautas are often a big family meal in my restaurants. Our Latin chefs are extremely creative in taking leftovers and making some of the most delicious food. To tell you the truth, I often will choose their flautas over my fanciest menu items.

3 tablespoons vegetable oil, plus more for frying

6 boneless chicken thighs

Salt

1 tablespoon cumin

1 tablespoon coriander

1 tablespoon cayenne

1 onion, thinly sliced

6 cloves garlic, thinly sliced

3 red Fresno chilies, seeded and chopped

3 tablespoons tomato paste

4 ancho chilies, soaked in hot water

2 chipotles in adobo

1. Heat a large Dutch oven over medium-high heat and add 3 tablespoons oil. Season the chicken with salt, cumin, coriander, and cayenne. Add the chicken to the pot and cook until golden brown, 3 minutes per side. Remove the chicken from the pot and set aside on a plate.

2. Add the onion, garlic, and Fresno chilies, and sauté for 3 minutes. Add the tomato paste and cook for another minute.

Chilies: the miracle medicine

The chilies found in Mexican food have fiber and important vitamins. Capsaicin (the hot part) helps boost metabolism and is associated with lowering cholesterol. I think it's one of the reasons that real Mexican food is so good for you.

12 6-inch flour tortillas

2 cups Cotija cheese

1 bunch cilantro (leaves only)

Sour cream, for garnish

Lime wedges, for garnish

SPECIAL EQUIPMENT:

Toothpicks

3. Remove the ancho peppers from the water, puree with the chipotles, and add to the pot, reserving the soaking liquid.

4. Place the chicken back into the pot and add some of the reserved soaking liquid. Cook the chicken until tender, about 45 minutes.

5. Remove the chicken from the sauce and shred when cool enough to handle. Add a little of the sauce to the chicken so that it is coated but not too wet, and set aside the remaining sauce.

6. Place 2 tablespoons of the chicken into a warmed flour tortilla. Add a little cheese and cilantro. Roll the tortilla up and fasten with a toothpick. Repeat with the remaining tortillas.

7. Heat 2 inches of oil in a large cast-iron skillet to about 350 °F. Place the tortillas into the oil seam-side down, and, working in batches, fry until golden brown on each side, about 2 minutes per side. Remove to a towel-lined plate to drain. Remove the toothpicks, and serve with the remaining sauce, sour cream, cilantro, lime wedges, and cheese.

Mama T shares her family secrets with Mario.

EGGPLANT PARMIGIANINO

SERVES 8 | Skill Level: EASY | Cook Time: 50 mins. | Prep Time: 15 mins. | Cost: $

This recipe reminds me of my childhood, because my grandfather, who was Italian, had this amazing garden with wonderful eggplants. When it came time to pick them, we would get the whole family together and set up an assembly line. Pop, as I called my grandfather, would slice the eggplants. Then my sister and I would dredge them in flour, egg, and bread. My dad would fry the slices in olive oil. Finally, Mom layered the slices in a dish with tomato sauce and cheese. About half an hour later, we were in eggplant heaven.

2 cups all-purpose flour

Salt

Pepper

5 large eggs

3½ cups Italian bread crumbs

1 cup freshly grated Parmigiano-Reggiano

¾ cup olive oil, plus more if needed

3 medium eggplants, sliced lengthwise into ¼-inch slices

4 cups Mario's Basic Tomato Sauce (page 30)

1 pound fresh mozzarella, thinly sliced

1. Preheat the oven to 350 °F.

2. Stir together the flour, salt, and pepper in a large dish, and set aside. Lightly beat the eggs in a high-sided dish, and set aside. Stir together the bread crumbs and ⅓ cup Parmigiano-Reggiano in a shallow dish.

3. Heat a small amount of oil in a large nonstick skillet to medium-high heat.

4. Working with 1 slice at a time, dredge each eggplant slice in the flour mixture, shaking off excess, then dip in the egg, letting excess drip off. Dredge in the bread crumb mixture until evenly coated. Transfer the eggplant directly to hot oil.

5. Fry the eggplant 4 slices at a time, turning over once, until golden brown, 5–6 minutes per batch. Transfer with tongs to paper towels to drain. Season with salt immediately after frying.

6. Spread 1 cup tomato sauce in the bottom of a 9-by-13-inch baking dish. Arrange about a third of the eggplant slices in one layer over the sauce, overlapping slightly if necessary. Cover the eggplant with about a third of the remaining sauce and a third of the mozzarella. Continue layering with the remaining eggplant, sauce, and mozzarella. Sprinkle top with remaining Parmigiano-Reggiano.

7. Bake uncovered, until cheese is melted and golden and sauce is bubbling, 30–35 minutes.

To salt or not to salt

Some people like to salt their eggplant slices and let them sit for a while before cooking. Mario said this practice comes from an old superstition that because eggplant (like the tomato) is a member of the nightshade family, it is poisonous, and the salt somehow "unpoisons" it. Well, that's just not so. What salting does is it removes water. I don't think it's a necessary step, but if you were brought up that way, be my guest. I find that leaving it unsalted and then baking makes for a more tender result.

STUFFED MUSHROOMS

MAKES 20 | **Skill Level: EASY** | **Cook Time: 30 mins.** | **Prep Time: 15 mins.** | **Cost: $**

I made these for Thanksgiving as an appetizer that's special but not super heavy with cheesy, bacon-y calories. They don't skimp on flavor, though. Mushrooms are light, but they have that special taste called "umami" that satisfies you like a piece of beef. Some people like to fry their stuffed mushrooms, but I find if you fill them up with fresh herbs and onions sautéed to the point of creaminess, then you can just bake them in the oven and save yourself 100 calories. And who doesn't want to save 100 calories . . . especially at Thanksgiving? Oh, and did I mention they cost about twenty-seven cents apiece? It occurs to me that if enough people eat stuffed mushrooms we can solve our national weight crisis and pay down the national debt, all with the help of this one hors d'oeuvre.

20 button mushrooms, scrubbed clean and stems reserved

3 tablespoons olive oil

2 tablespoons shallots, minced

1 large clove garlic, minced

2 tablespoons almonds, chopped

Salt, to taste

3 tablespoons parsley, chopped

1 teaspoon herbes de Provence or dried thyme

2 tablespoons whole wheat bread crumbs

2–3 tablespoons vegetable stock

2 tablespoons Pecorino cheese, grated

1. Preheat the oven to 375 °F.

2. Finely chop the mushroom stems. Heat 1 tablespoon olive oil in a small nonstick skillet over medium-high heat. Sauté the chopped mushroom stems and the shallots for 4–5 minutes, stirring often.

3. Add the garlic and almonds, and season with salt. Stir well and sauté 2 more minutes. Turn off the heat and add the parsley, herbes de Provence (or thyme), and whole wheat bread crumbs.

4. Pour the vegetable stock into a food processor, then the rest of the stuffing. Pulse several times to get a fine mixture, almost a paste.

5. Toss the mushroom caps with olive oil. Fill each mushroom with the stuffing. Sprinkle grated Pecorino cheese over each mushroom and bake for 20–25 minutes, until the cheese browns a little and the mushrooms are warmed through.

FALL

Making it look like spaghetti

If you are not familiar with spaghetti squash, the way you get those spaghetti-like strands is to roast the squash and then remove the cooked flesh of the squash by scraping it with a fork.

SPAGHETTI SQUASH FRITTERS

SERVES 6 | **Skill Level: MODERATE** | **Cook Time: 35–40 mins.** | **Cost: $**

Spaghetti squash fritters, with blue cheese and nutmeg in the batter, are an intensely flavorful and ecstatically crispy appetizer or side. Just like potato latkes (pancakes) are a special treat at Hanukkah, these fritters at Thanksgiving or Christmas have that same hot, savory crispness that pretty much guarantees your guests will eat every one. If it's anything like my house, they'll start to hover around the fryer, barely able to wait until you take them from the hot oil.

1 medium spaghetti squash

1½ tablespoons fresh sage, chopped, plus whole leaves for garnish

⅛ teaspoon whole nutmeg, grated

1 scallion (green and white parts), thinly sliced on the bias

2 teaspoons garlic, minced

1 teaspoon kosher salt or coarse sea salt

½ teaspoon freshly ground pepper

4 ounces blue cheese, coarsely chopped or crumbled

Zest of 1 orange

1 large egg

3–4 tablespoons all-purpose flour

Canola oil, for deep-frying

1. Preheat the oven to 400 °F.

2. Cut the squash in half and remove the seeds. Season with salt and roast on a foil-lined half sheet pan for 30 minutes, until tender. Let cool. With a fork, scrape the squash to remove long strands and place on a towel.

3. Wrap the spaghetti squash in a kitchen towel and wring as much liquid out of it as possible, discarding the liquid.

4. In a medium bowl, combine the squash, chopped sage, nutmeg, scallion, garlic, salt, pepper, blue cheese, and all but 1 teaspoon of the orange zest. Stir in the egg and flour, and mix well until combined.

5. Add the canola oil to a large shallow pan two-thirds up the sides of the pan. Place the pan over medium-high heat. The oil should be heated to 360 °F for frying.

6. Drop spoonfuls of the squash mixture into the oil. Cook until the fritters are golden brown, about 4 minutes. After the fritters have cooked for 2 to 3 minutes, add some fresh sage leaves, but be careful because they will pop. Fry the sage leaves for a couple of minutes and remove with the fritters. Drain the fried fritters and sage leaves on paper towels and season with salt.

7. Transfer the fritters to plates and garnish with the reserved orange zest and fried sage leaves.

Sage advice

About 45 seconds before the fritters are done, put a bunch of sage leaves in the oil. Fried sage is a terrific garnish, and the flavor it releases into the frying oil (and then into the fritters) creates an insanely appetizing aroma.

WINE-STAINED PASTA WITH SAUSAGE MEATBALLS AND CAULIFLOWER

SERVES 6 | **Skill Level: EASY** | **Cook Time: 25–30 mins.** | **Prep Time: 15 mins.** | **Cost: $**

People are always blown away when I make this dish. Cooking your pasta in a whole bottle of inexpensive wine looks great, sounds brave, tastes amazing. For those of you who are hoping to get a little extra buzz from your pasta, sorry to be a buzzkill, but the alcohol just about cooks off by the time the pasta is ready. I made this on the show when Jimmy Fallon visited. Jimmy couldn't resist busting my chops with a story about the time we were in Ireland to play some golf and I took him to a market to shop for ingredients for dinner. I asked him to find a grill pan, and he comes back with one and told me there was a whole Mario Batali kitchenware aisle in the store.

"It's like going to buy Sam Adams beer with the real Sam Adams!" he said. Jimmy got extra-special pleasure making me, Mario Batali, pay for the Mario Batali grill pan. Double extra pleasure in making me relive the whole scene by telling the audience about it.

1 bottle plus 1 cup inexpensive red wine

2½ pounds sweet Italian sausage, casings removed

¼ cup extra virgin olive oil

1 medium head cauliflower, cut into small florets

2 cloves garlic, sliced

Pinch of red pepper flakes

2 cups Mario's Basic Tomato Sauce (recipe follows)

1½ pounds garganelli pasta

2 tablespoons salt

1 cup freshly grated Pecorino Romano, to serve

1. Fill a large pot with half water and half wine and bring to a boil.

2. Using your hands, form the sausage into small meatballs, about the size of marbles. In a 12- to 14-inch sauté pan, heat the oil over medium heat, until just smoking. Add the sausage balls in two batches and sauté, rolling them around, until they are browned all over, 5–6 minutes per batch. Remove, and set aside on a plate.

3. Add the cauliflower to the pan and cook until soft, about 5 minutes. Add the garlic and the red pepper flakes, cook for another minute, and add the 1 cup red wine to the cauliflower. Bring to a boil, and then add the tomato sauce and sausage balls. Bring to a boil again. Then lower the heat to a simmer and cook for 5 minutes. Remove from the heat.

4. Drop the garganelli into the boiling wine/water, season heavily with salt, and cook for 1 minute less than the package instructions indicate. Just before the pasta is done, carefully ladle ½ cup of the cooking wine/water into the sausage mixture.

FALL

5. Drain the pasta in a colander and add it to the sausage mixture. Toss until pasta is nicely coated. Pour into a serving bowl and serve immediately, with the grated Pecorino on the side.

MARIO'S BASIC TOMATO SAUCE

¼ cup extra virgin olive oil

1 yellow onion, diced

5 garlic cloves, peeled and thinly sliced

3 tablespoons fresh thyme, leaves only

½ medium carrot, shredded

2 28-ounce cans peeled whole tomatoes crushed by hand and juices reserved

Salt, to taste

1. In a 3-quart saucepan, heat the olive oil over medium heat. Add the onion and garlic and cook until soft and light golden brown, about 8 to 10 minutes.

2. Add the thyme and carrot and cook 5 minutes more, until the carrot is quite soft.

3. Add the tomatoes and juice and bring to a boil, stirring often. Lower the heat and simmer for 30 minutes until as thick as hot cereal.

4. Season with salt and serve.

Mario and Jimmy Fallon after a round of stovetop Ping Pong.

GENERAL TSO'S CHICKEN

SERVES 4 | Skill Level: EASY | Cook Time: 20–25 mins. | Prep Time: 10 mins. | Cost: $

There was a restaurant in my hometown, Port Jefferson Station, Long Island, that made me a lifelong convert to the good general's namesake chicken. Actually, in the balloon-popping department, it is my moral duty to inform you that as far as anyone can tell, there was no General Tso. The name originated from confusion with the Chinese word for "ancestral meeting house." Somehow I can't imagine anyone ordering a quart of ancestral meeting house chicken to go. So General Tso's it is. My homemade version is crispy, sweet, and uses lots less fat and salt.

FOR THE SAUCE:

1 tablespoon cornstarch

½ cup cold water

4 cloves garlic, sliced

2 tablespoons fresh ginger, grated

3 tablespoons honey

2 tablespoons low-sodium soy sauce

3 tablespoons Chinese rice wine

1 tablespoon red pepper flakes

FOR THE CHICKEN:

3 tablespoons cornstarch

½ teaspoon salt

¼ teaspoon pepper

2 tablespoons vegetable oil

1 pound boneless, skinless chicken breasts, cut into 1-inch pieces

1 pound broccoli florets, blanched

1½ cups white rice, cooked according to package instructions

4 scallions (greens only), thinly sliced, for garnish

1 teaspoon sesame seeds, for garnish

1. For the sauce, in a large bowl, mix together 1 tablespoon cornstarch and cold water until smooth. Add the garlic, ginger, honey, soy sauce, Chinese rice wine, and red pepper flakes. Set aside.

2. In a separate bowl, mix the cornstarch, salt, and pepper together until combined. Add the chicken and toss until coated.

3. Heat a large nonstick skillet with vegetable oil. Shake excess coating off the chicken and cook until golden, 4–6 minutes.

4. Add the sauce mixture and cook until the sauce has thickened. Add the steamed broccoli and toss to coat with the sauce.

5. Plate with rice. Add the scallions and sesame seeds for garnish.

ROASTED CHICKEN WITH SWEET POTATOES AND SAGE

SERVES 6 | **Skill Level: MODERATE** | **Cook Time: 1 hr.** | **Prep Time: 15 mins.** | **Cost: $**

Ask any professional chef what the measure of a great restaurant is and many will answer, "A roasted chicken." Brown and crispy on the outside, juicy and suc-culent meat on the inside, and a panful of roasted, caramelized vegetables. A house with a roasted chicken in the oven says, "This is a place where people love food." For me, the key is salting liberally, inside and out, the night before. Studies have shown that the salt permeates the flesh of the chicken and keeps it from drying out in the oven. My wife, Lizzie, and I make this once a week and never tire of it.

1 3- to 4-pound chicken

Salt

1 stick butter, room temperature

1 small bunch fresh sage, chopped

1 onion, peeled

2 celery roots, peeled and cubed

3 sweet potatoes, cubed

3 tablespoons cumin seeds

Drizzle of olive oil

Pepper

1. A day before cooking, rinse the chicken inside and out under cold water and pat dry. Salt it liberally, cover, and re-frigerate. Remove the chicken from the refrigerator an hour before cooking it. Preheat the oven to 425 °F.

2. Combine butter and sage, and rub under the skin. Put the onion in the cavity of the chicken.

3. Toss the celery roots, potatoes, cumin seeds, olive oil, salt, and pepper.

4. Put the chicken in an ovenproof sauté pan or in a roast-ing pan, breast side up, on top of the sweet potato and cel-ery root mixture. Slide it into the oven, and roast it until the thigh reaches 160 °F or until the juices run clear, about 1 hour.

5. Remove from the oven and let rest for 10–20 minutes. Cut the chicken into 8 pieces and serve with the vegetables.

Even ugly vegetables taste great

Depending on the season, I like to surround the chicken with a bed of vegetable chunks. Celery root—which gets the ugly prize—cooks up soft and sweet. Potatoes and sweet potatoes are crispy on the outside and creamy within. Onions and garlic get a golden half-crispy, half-melty soft sweetness. Just remember: the chicken takes nearly an hour to cook, so you want your vegetable pieces pretty big. That way they cook at the same rate as the chicken.

Better with butter

Add some fresh sage to soft butter and massage the skin with it. Also work some of the butter-sage mix under the skin. It keeps the meat moist, adds a deep nutty flavor, and produces a beautiful golden-brown skin.

Think twice, it's all right

It takes very little extra to roast two chickens instead of one. Then you have a week's worth of leftovers for salads, potpies, etc., or simply reheat and serve with your favorite condiments and sauces, from plain old mustard to pesto to Sriracha.

Michael gives a big hug to his one and only love, Liz.

CAST-IRON PORK PIE

| SERVES 6 | Skill Level: EASY | Cook Time: 25–30 mins. | Prep Time: 10 mins. | Cost: $ |

One of our favorite things around the Symon household is a savory pie. I have been making a pork pie for years, but when I read Keith Richards's autobiography, he gave me a new idea when he talked about how the Rolling Stones grew up in households where shepherd's pie, with its distinctive mashed potato crust, was a go-to meal. Hey, if it's cool enough for Keith, it's definitely cool enough for me. Then I wanted to health it up a little, so I included a good helping of kale. Daphne loved that idea. Anytime you can get a green leafy vegetable into a recipe, you've got a happy Daphne. And, of course, some melted Cheddar cheese on top . . . because Cheddar cheese is so good on apple pie, I figured it could go into my reinvented pork pie.

½ pound bacon, medium diced

2 pounds ground pork

Drizzle of olive oil

2 large onions

2 cups kale, roughly chopped

1 cup celery, chopped

2 cloves garlic, chopped

Pinch of ground cinnamon

Large pinch of salt

Pinch of pepper

Pinch of ground nutmeg

½ cup fresh parsley, chopped

½ cup celery leaves, chopped

3 cups mashed potatoes

1 cup aged Cheddar, grated

1. Preheat the oven to 450 °F.

2. In a cast-iron skillet, brown the bacon and pork. Remove from the pan and reserve.

3. To the same pan, add a drizzle of olive oil, onions, kale, celery, garlic, cinnamon, salt, pepper, and nutmeg, and sweat for 4-5 minutes, then add the pork and bacon back to the pan with a splash of water. Mix, then add the parsley and celery leaves, and stir in to combine. Remove from heat.

4. Spread the mashed potatoes over the pork mixture and sprinkle with grated Cheddar.

5. Bake until golden brown, about 15–20 minutes, garnish with celery leaves, and serve.

Daphne says

If you want to do a vegetarian version of this dish, eggplant, any fall squash, maybe even some portabella mushrooms will work beautifully. And, yes, don't forget the kale. Love that kale!

Straighten up and fry right

If you like to fry, get one of those home fryers with a temperature control. They take a lot of the fear out of frying, because you know your oil is always at the right temperature. If you aren't in the mood for another gadget, you can always fry in a skillet. Just remember that when things fry, the hot fat tends to burble up. To keep it from overflowing and maybe burning yourself in the process, I recommend that the oil come no more than two-thirds of the way up the pan.

Daphne's healthy hint

Frying has been getting a bad reputation that it doesn't deserve. If you fry at the right temperature and drain your fried food well, fats like olive and canola oil are actually quite healthful. Fats help your body to make use of the antioxidants in fresh vegetables. When frying, make sure you don't heat the oil until it smokes, because if you do, the fat breaks down and you lose all those healthy free radicals.

CRISPY LIME AND CILANTRO CHICKEN WINGS

SERVES 6 | Skill Level: EASY | Cook Time: 30–35 mins. | Prep Time: 20 mins.
Inactive Prep Time: 2–3 hrs. | Cost: $–$$ Cost will depend on which fat you use to fry.

Everyone loves Buffalo chicken wings. Me too. It's a perfect football-watching food. But crispy cooked wings with a delicious mix of flavors don't begin and end with the blue cheese, butter, and vinegar version of the sauce that has become a game-day mainstay. My recipe comes from my hometown in the Midwest via a marinade and dipping sauce with the bright, spicy, tangy flavors of Asia. You give up none of the powerhouse flavor of traditional Buffalo wings, but it's a much lighter dish, so you can eat more without filling up. If you are watching this when your team is playing, remember that if they score on a sixty-yard fumble recovery, don't swallow the bone while you are cheering madly.

FOR THE MARINADE:

1 tablespoon kosher salt

1 teaspoon sugar

1 tablespoon smoked paprika

Juice and zest of 2 limes (reserve zest for the wing sauce)

½ cup extra virgin olive oil

3 pounds chicken wings

4 cups duck fat or vegetable oil, for frying

FOR THE WING SAUCE:

½ cup hot sauce (such as Sriracha)

1 tablespoon apple cider vinegar

2–3 tablespoons honey

3 tablespoons unsalted butter

Reserved lime zest

½ teaspoon salt

½ cup cilantro leaves

Lime wedges, to garnish

2 jalapeños, thinly sliced, to garnish

1. In a large bowl, combine the ingredients for the marinade. Add the chicken wings, and toss to coat. Cover and marinate in the refrigerator for 2–3 hours.

2. Preheat the oven to 350 °F. Spread the wings out on a baking sheet with sides. Pour over any remaining marinade, and bake for 15–20 minutes, until just cooked through. Remove from the oven and let cool slightly, about 5 minutes.

3. Place a high-sided cast-iron pan over medium-high heat and add the duck fat or vegetable oil. Using a deep-fry thermometer to monitor the temperature, allow the fat to heat to 360 °F.

4. Carefully add the wings to the oil in batches and fry until golden brown and crispy, about 4 minutes per batch. Drain on a paper towel–lined plate and season them with salt.

5. To make the wing sauce, place a medium saucepan over medium heat. Add all the ingredients and whisk until the butter has melted, then taste and season with salt.

6. Place the chicken wings in a large bowl and pour the sauce over the top. Toss to coat the wings with the sauce. Add in the cilantro leaves, tossing one more time. Serve with lime wedges and sliced jalapeños.

FALL

Thanksgiving—
The Familiest Day

Clinton

THANKSGIVING IS SUPER IMPORTANT TO ME as a time for the entire family to get together. It's always a group project. Nobody is expected to do all the work. Someone would volunteer for vegetables. Someone else for turkey. Still another for dessert. Without a lot a planning, somehow it was naturally coordinated. We all ended up having a great time without sticking Mom in the kitchen by herself for 8 hours. And don't let me forget cleanup. It's like a military process. When the meal is done—boom!—everybody gets up with five things in their hands and it all goes on an assembly line for the SWAT team in the kitchen. Thanksgiving is one of the few times when cleaning up after is actually fun! Maybe the only time.

Daphne

WE ARE A FAIRLY LARGE CLAN and we do something called the Oz Family Turkey Bowl, because, of course, my dad—Mr. Healthy—had to find a way to work activity and exercise into the biggest eating day of the year. So we get twenty-five people together and have ten-on-ten full-contact football with five subs for the people who, inevitably, pull a muscle or get a scrape. To give you some idea of how seriously we take this, my mother played this game when she was eight months pregnant with me. Of course we have a real turkey, but we also have a tofu turkey, or, as we call it, a Tofurkey.

Carla

BACK IN THE DAY (when I was in business for myself), we didn't have much money and I usually didn't have much of a Thanksgiving anyway since the holidays were big work days. One year, I decided to have my own Thanksgiving and I wanted to treat myself. My girlfriend Greta and I bought this beautiful china . . . like *totally gorgeous*, not to mention *very expensive*. We picked a few different patterns, a beautiful tablecloth. We invited people over—mostly holiday stragglers with nowhere else to go. Dinner was super—six or seven courses. It was a special night.

Michael

THANKSGIVING IS MY FAVORITE HOLIDAY of the year by far. It's all about food, family, friends, and football. Which is good. My grandfather used to do it, but we took over in the past couple of years. All our families are there plus people who work for us who are too far from their families to drive home. So it can be anywhere between twenty-five and fifty people at our house, so it is truly a feast. We have one ginormous table where we seat about twenty-eight to thirty people, and the kids sit at another one. Quite a spectacle!

Mario

I HAD A BIG FAMILY with lots of cousins on both the eastern side of Washington State and the western side of the state, so we kind of alternated hosting duties every year. We would go to either Aunt Izzy's or Aunt Mari's or Aunt Cheri's or Uncle Paul's or our house. And every one of the holidays, whether it was July Fourth or Christmas or New Year's Day or Easter or any of them, including Thanksgiving, got divvied up in some secret meeting that I never knew existed. Day of, we all just knew where we were going. We'd figure out with the cousins what kind of mischief we might get in before dinner, including some football. And then we would just have this fabulous turkey. Because of our round-robin hosting, each family would have three or four years to warm up for the next time they were on duty, so it was always just a little bit different.

Setting the Thanksgiving Table

THANKSGIVING ISN'T JUST ABOUT THE FOOD. It's also about dressing: the turkey, the table, and you. And remember: dressing doesn't have to mean dressy. So here are two approaches to your Thanksgiving tabletop: one dressy and one a little more down home.

Casual thursday

If you are like me, you like hosting but you don't want to carry the whole burden on your shoulders, so you divvy up the work. Someone brings the stuffing, someone else the pumpkin pie, maybe your cousin brings the Brussels sprouts, and the lazybones in the crowd gets to open a can of cranberry sauce. Okay, a nice bunch of recipes, but the dishes they bring them in are a mix and match, hodgepodge. It doesn't look cohesive.

My advice is to map out the buffet. I like to use different heights to my advantage. All the veggies on one level, maybe the stuffings and mashed potatoes on another, a big turkey platter on another, and pies and cakes on another. So even if the serving dishes look different, each course gets its own level.

Now how are you going to make those levels? Stack books for each different level and cover them with gift paper, place mats, or decorative cloth remnants. Just like that, your spread has a cool design theme, and the eye is drawn to each grouping.

If the look of everyone's casseroles and platters is just too mixed up for you, use your own plates and presentation platters.

Dress-up day

My biggest piece of advice for a formal table is to keep it white and simple. No colors to match, just elegant simplicity. Use white linens and white napkins. And for Pete's sake, iron your tablecloth. Nothing ruins a table like a big crease that runs down the center of it. I'm a freak. I love to iron to relax myself. I do. I can get five shirts done in 7 minutes. I get into the Zen ironing moment, where I feel like I can do just anything while I'm ironing. I talk to people, I watch television; it's my favorite thing. But enough about me. Okay.

I'm nuts about nuts and ape for apples

Autumn fruits and vegetables add color that is literally appetizing to a table. Apples, pomegranates, nuts . . . are beautiful . . . and delicious.

Get set

The other thing you really have to do is pay attention to how you're setting the table. There is a format for your silverware and your plates. Let's all go through this together. It is fork, fork, plate, knife, spoon.

C'mon say it with me: "Fork, fork, plate, knife, spoon."

Then the water glass goes over the knife and the wineglass goes over the spoon.

Where does the water glass go?
Say it with me: "Over the knife."
Where does the wineglass go?
Say it with me: "Over the spoon."

And then your dessert fork and your coffee spoon go above the plate. I'm not going to make you say it again. But the reason for this is when you're done with the main course and you have dessert in front of you, all you have to do is reach out and your fork and spoon are right at your fingertips.

I was framed

Ordinary ninety-nine-cent picture frames with your guests' pictures in them are a thoughtful and effective place card. People never get tired of looking at themselves.

Set the people too

It's nice to tell people where to sit, because you never want to have your best conversationalists clustered together. Spread them out. If you have a bunch of duds on one side, fuggedaboutit.

The takeaway

One thing that makes a dinner memorable is a memento to take home. Around holiday time, a Christmas ornament is pretty and colorful. It's one of the two things that almost everyone likes. The other is fireworks. My advice: stay away from things that explode.

LEMON SAGE TURKEY

SERVES 10 to 14 | **Skill Level: EASY** | **Cook Time: 3–3 ½ hrs.** | **Prep Time: 20 mins.** | **Cost: $**
Inactive Prep Time: 12 hrs.

I've been eating my family's turkey for a long time. It's good, but I thought I could come up with something better . . . fresher . . . more flavorful and, most of all, moist. So, Kelly family, here's my take on turkey. I call it Lemon Sage Turkey. It's actually a lemon, sage, and garlic turkey, but lemon sage sounds more zingy to me. Aside from a good turkey—free range and organic get my vote—there are three secrets to my big bird. First, you have to brine. Not everyone believes in brining. In fact, Michael is a devout non-brining crusader, but it makes for juicier white meat.

The second secret is the compound butter of lemon and garlic. You rub it over and inside the skin and it becomes a delicious crust-helper and meat-moistener.

Finally, stuffing all those lemons in the cavity freshens everything, and the scent of the lemon oil makes a great little accent.

FOR THE BRINE:

1 gallon water

1 cup sea salt

1 bunch fresh rosemary

1 bunch sage

1 bunch fresh thyme

2 cups maple syrup

10 cloves garlic, smashed, skin on

1 gallon ice water

2 cups apple cider

MARIO'S BRINE

1. In a large stockpot, combine the water, sea salt, rosemary, sage, thyme, maple syrup, and garlic cloves. Bring to a boil, and stir frequently to be sure salt is dissolved. Remove from heat, and let cool to room temperature.

2. When the broth mixture is cool, pour it into a clean 5-gallon bucket. Stir in the ice water and cider.

3. Place the turkey, breast down, into the brine. Make sure that the cavity gets filled. Place the bucket in the refrigerator overnight but no longer than 12 hours.

4. Remove the turkey, carefully drain off the excess brine, and pat dry. Discard excess brine.

FOR THE TURKEY:

1 12- to 16-pound turkey

2 sticks unsalted butter at room temperature

1 shallot, finely minced

1 clove garlic, finely minced

3 tablespoons sage, minced, plus 1 bunch fresh sage

4 lemons

Kosher salt, to taste

Freshly ground black pepper, to taste

2 tablespoons olive oil

1. Preheat the oven to 425 °F. Arrange an oven shelf in the lower third of the oven.

2. Let the turkey come to room temperature. Remove the neck and giblets from the body and neck cavities, and reserve them for turkey broth. Drain the juices, and pat the bird dry inside and out.

3. Meanwhile, make the compound butter. In a large bowl, combine room temperature butter, shallot, garlic, minced sage, and juice and zest of 1 lemon. Stir together with a rubber spatula. Add salt and pepper to taste. Set aside.

4. Arrange the turkey breast side up in a rack (preferably a V-rack) set in a heavy, large roasting pan.

5. Season the inside of the turkey with salt and pepper to taste. Puncture two lemons with a fork and stuff inside cavity of the turkey, along with the fresh sage.

6. Carefully smooth the compound butter under the skin of the turkey, being mindful not to tear the membrane connecting the skin to the breast. Thinly slice the remaining lemon and slide slices under the skin along with butter.

7. Coat the outside of the bird with olive oil, and rub all over its skin. Season generously with kosher salt and freshly ground black pepper.

8. Roast the turkey in the lower third of the oven for 20 minutes at 425 °F. Then turn the oven down to 325 °F and roast until an instant-read thermometer inserted into the thickest part of the leg-thigh joint reads 165 °F.

9. Transfer the turkey to a platter, leaving the drippings in the pan for the gravy, and cover the turkey loosely with foil. Let the turkey rest for at least 20 minutes, preferably 30 minutes, before carving.

CHESTNUT MERGUEZ STUFFING

SERVES 6 | Skill Level: EASY | Cook Time: 50 mins. | Prep Time: 10 Mins. | Cost: $

One of the strongest Thanksgiving memories I have of growing up in my house is the aroma of roasting chestnuts. My grandma always roasted them for every holiday, and then we kids tried to figure out how to not eat them. We hid them in the couch, we put them behind her dresser. Now that I am a grown-up, I have altered my opinion of chestnuts. I love them, and to the best of my knowledge, my kids never hid them behind the furniture. I also like sausage in my stuffing, pretty much any sausage, but lately I have fallen in love with the slightly spicy North African lamb sausage known as merguez.

4 tablespoons extra virgin olive oil

1 pound merguez sausage, casings removed

1 large onion, diced

5 stalks celery, diced

1 cup chestnuts, roughly chopped

1 cup apples, peeled and diced

4 cups cornbread, toasted and cubed

1 tablespoon sage, for sprinkling

2½ cups chicken broth

½ cup butter, melted

1. In a large skillet over medium heat, heat the oil, then crumble the merguez into the pan and cook for 4 minutes. Add the onion, celery, chestnuts, and apples, and sauté, stirring occasionally, until sausage is cooked through.

2. In a large bowl, place the cubed cornbread. Add the sausage mixture, and sprinkle with the sage. Pour the broth and butter over the top, and toss to combine.

3. Spoon the mixture into a 9-by-13-inch baking dish and cover. Bake at 350 °F for 45 minutes.

Getting ready

Most people, the Batalis included, find themselves with too much to do and too little time when it comes to holiday meals. You can assemble this dressing/stuffing up to a day or two before it gets popped in the oven. Then on Turkey Day, put it into the oven for 45 minutes before you plan on serving your turkey.

Dressed or stuffed?

Some people call it dressing. Some call it stuffing. I learned that the difference is stuffing goes inside the bird and dressing gets cooked separately. Call it whatever you want, just so long as the family enjoys it.

MUSHROOM AND VEGETABLE STUFFING

SERVES 4 | **Skill Level: EASY** | **Cook Time: 45–50 mins.** | **Prep Time: 15 mins.** | **Cost: $**

At our family Thanksgiving, we serve a stuffing for meat eaters (turkey eaters count as carnivores) and a vegetarian stuffing. My veggie version has walnuts, apples, celery, and, most important, mushrooms. For those of you who think veggie stuffing is somehow second best, all I can say is we always run out of the vegetarian version first. It's hefty enough to satisfy like a classic dressing but way lighter on calories and fat.

½ loaf multigrain bread, torn into bite-sized pieces

1 tablespoon extra virgin olive oil

1 shallot, finely chopped

1 stalk celery, thinly sliced

½ pound shiitake mushrooms, stems removed and chopped

1 bunch kale, stems removed and cut into ribbons

Salt

Pepper

1 Granny Smith apple, cored and diced

1 clove garlic, minced

1 tablespoon fresh thyme leaves, minced

⅓ cup parsley leaves, minced

1 tablespoon fresh sage leaves, minced

½ cup walnuts, toasted and coarsely chopped

1 cup vegetable broth

1. In an oven preheated to 400 °F, bake the torn bread until crunchy, about 10 minutes.

2. Heat the extra virgin olive oil in a nonstick skillet over medium heat. Add the shallot, celery, mushrooms, and kale. Season with salt and pepper to taste. Cook for 5 minutes, stirring occasionally, and add the apple once the shallot has softened. Once the apple has softened, about 5 minutes, add the garlic, thyme, parsley, and sage. Cook for about a minute, until fragrant, then remove from heat, and mix in the walnuts and bread.

3. Add vegetable broth until moist but not soggy. Cover with foil and bake at 400 °F for 25 minutes. Remove foil, bake an additional 10 minutes, and serve.

The viewers speak

In a survey of *Chew* viewers, we asked people what was their favorite part of Thanksgiving: 50 percent said spending time with family and friends, 40 percent said cooking, and 10 percent said cleaning up, to which we answered, "What's up with that?" But when you think about it, the deep dishing (as in gossip) really gets good with the water running, everybody full and happy (and maybe lubricated with some cocktails and wine). If you want to be a fly on the wall, the cleanup kitchen is the wall for you.

PAN-SEARED TURKEY WITH GREMOLATA

SERVES 6 | Skill Level: EASY | Cook Time: 1–1 ½ hrs. | Prep Time: 10 mins. | Cost: $

Inactive Prep Time: 12 hrs.

I might never have come up with this recipe if my car hadn't broken down on the way to a catering job. My client was looking forward to my cooking turkey at her home. She was psyched about the house filling up with the aroma of it roasting in the oven. Well, it took so long to get the car fixed that by the time I arrived at her house, I wouldn't have been able to cook and serve dinner until very late. And then I remembered how often I had been told that you can think of a turkey as a big chicken, so I cut it into parts: wing, drumstick, thigh, breast. It cut down the cooking time by two-thirds, and everyone really liked the way we rescued Thanksgiving.

FOR THE BRINING LIQUID:

4 cups water

½–¾ cup kosher salt

½ cup brown sugar

10 whole allspice

10 whole cloves

10 whole black peppercorns

5 star anise

7–8 sprigs thyme

½ cup olive oil

1 12- to 15-pound turkey, cut into 8 pieces

FOR THE SPICY GREMOLATA:

1½ cups packed flat-leaf parsley

¼ cup sage leaves

4 cloves garlic, smashed

3 tablespoons lemon zest

2 teaspoons crushed red pepper flakes

2 teaspoons kosher salt

½ cup olive oil

1. Combine all the brining ingredients in a large resealable plastic bag, and shake to dissolve the salt and sugar. Place the turkey parts in the bag, and place in the refrigerator for 6 hours or overnight.

2. Remove the turkey from the brine and rinse thoroughly. Pat dry. Gently loosen the skin from the turkey pieces. Combine the spicy gremolata ingredients and liberally rub the gremolata under the skin on each part.

3. Preheat the oven to 400 °F. Heat a heavy skillet to medium-high heat. Sear each piece until golden brown on all sides. Place seared pieces on a sheet pan, and finish cooking them in the oven. Cook for 1–1½ hours until all the pieces have an internal temperature of 170 °F.

Special bonus . . . shelf space!

If you're the one making Thanksgiving, no doubt you are familiar with the problem of too much food in too small of a refrigerator. Breaking the turkey down in smaller parts is a much more compact way to store it overnight. That should help with your space problem, although refrigerators, just like people, tend to get overstuffed at holiday time.

BRUSSELS SPROUTS À LA "RUSS" WITH WALNUTS AND CAPERS

| SERVES 5 | Skill Level: EASY | Cook Time: 5 mins. | Prep Time: 5 mins. | Cost: $ |

I think one of the reasons I started doing 5-in-5 is my father-in-law, Russ. Whenever I am making Thanksgiving dinner—in fact, whenever I am in the kitchen making anything—Russ will wander into the kitchen and start picking off the plate. My way to deal with this is to get as much done as I can before he shows. Then I chill out until we're ready to make last-minute dishes.

Brussels sprouts are one of my favorite vegetables for Thanksgiving. In most of the country, they're one of the few green vegetables that you can still buy fresh and locally. Many people have included them on their Thanksgiving menu, roasting them in the oven, maybe with some diced apples and bacon. I prefer to fry them. They get very golden brown outside. Their sugars come out and get rid of any funky cabbage-y bitterness.

Canola oil, for deep-frying

½ serrano chili, seeded and minced

1½ teaspoons honey

2 tablespoons red wine vinegar

1 tablespoon extra virgin olive oil

Salt, to taste

Pepper, to taste

½ pound Brussels sprouts, trimmed and quartered lengthwise

1 tablespoon capers

¼ cup walnut pieces, toasted

1. Pour enough oil into a medium pot so that the oil comes two-thirds up the sides. Heat to 350 °F.

2. While the oil is heating, whisk together the serrano, honey, red wine vinegar, and extra virgin olive oil in a bowl large enough to toss all the Brussels sprouts. Season with salt and pepper to taste. Keep the bowl near the stovetop.

3. Fry the Brussels sprouts until the edges begin to curl and brown, about 2–3 minutes. Carefully add the capers and stand back, because they tend to splatter a bit. Fry for another minute. Remove the Brussels sprouts and the capers directly to the bowl with the vinaigrette. Toss to coat. Add salt and pepper to taste, and toss in the toasted walnuts.

Sweet and salty

Whenever I cook anything sweet, I like to put a good pinch of salt in it. It helps bring out the flavors, balancing sweet and savory. You'd be surprised how much fuller a sweet thing tastes when it gets some help in the salt department.

CHOCOLATE PUMPKIN PIE

SERVES 8 | **Skill Level: EASY** | **Cook Time: 1–1 ½ hrs.** | **Prep Time: 20 mins.** | **Cost: $**

Inactive Prep Time: 1 hr.

I would rather have Thanksgiving without turkey than to skip pumpkin pie. It's my favorite thing. Carla tells me people feel that way about sweet potato pie in the South, but I'm a pumpkin guy all the way. I can't imagine doing without it. But, being the kind of chef that I am, you know how I like to take traditional recipes and give them a little twist. Well, here we have a pumpkin pie enriched with rich melted chocolate. A new classic, if I do say so myself.

FOR THE CRUST:

1¼ cups all-purpose flour

2 teaspoons salt

½ teaspoon sugar

½ cup unsalted butter, very cold and cut into small pieces

2–3 tablespoons ice-cold water

FOR THE FILLING:

3 ounces bittersweet chocolate, very finely chopped

6 ounces semisweet chocolate, chopped

4 tablespoons unsalted butter, cut into small pieces

1 14-ounce can pumpkin puree

1 12-ounce can evaporated milk

¾ cup packed light brown sugar

3 large eggs

1 tablespoon cornstarch

1 teaspoon vanilla extract

¼ teaspoon salt

¾ teaspoon ground cinnamon

¾ teaspoon ground ginger

¼ teaspoon ground nutmeg

Pinch of ground cloves

Whipped cream, to serve

TO MAKE THE CRUST:

1. Combine the flour, salt, sugar, and butter in a food processor and pulse until coarse, with small marbles of butter remaining. Sprinkle in 2 tablespoons of the ice water, and pulse until crumbly and the dough holds when squeezed together. Add another sprinkle of water if too dry, but do not overmix.

2. Transfer the dough to a plastic zip-top bag, press into a disc, and refrigerate for 1 hour.

3. Preheat the oven to 425 °F.

4. Roll out the dough on a floured surface. Press into a pie plate and trim, leaving 1 inch excess around the edges. Fold under and flute the edges. Cut a piece of parchment or non-stick foil to the size of the pie, and use it to line the piecrust. Fill with pie weights or dried beans, and bake until golden, about 15 minutes.

5. Reduce heat to 325 °F.

TO MAKE THE FILLING:

6. In a double boiler, melt the bittersweet chocolate, semisweet chocolate, and butter, stirring frequently until smooth, and remove from heat.

7. In a large bowl, mix together the pumpkin puree, evaporated milk, light brown sugar, eggs, cornstarch, vanilla, salt, cinnamon, ginger, nutmeg, and cloves. Fold in the chocolate mixture, and pour into the piecrust. Place the pie pan on a baking sheet. Bake at 325 °F until center of pie has set, about an hour. Cool completely to serve with whipped cream.

FALL

BATTER FRIED APPLE RINGS

| MAKES 8 TO 10 | Skill Level: EASY | Cook Time: 15 mins. | Prep Time: 10 mins. | Cost: $ |

There are few things I like better than going back to an old family recipe and making something new and delicious from it. A few months ago, I was at home going through one of those boxes that you promise yourself that you're going to sort through but you never do. I'm glad I did, because right there in my hot little hands was a Betty Crocker box. Every month we'd get a new packet of recipes, and over the years they added up to a boxful of happiness for me. The recipe for apple pancakes got me thinking. I added in some pumpkin pie spices to give it more Thanksgiving spirit. Then I reduced some apple cider down until it was thick and sweet enough to call it syrup, and I poured it over granny smith apple fritters that I fried in my favorite childhood pancake batter. When Daphne saw how much apple was included in the recipe, she said, "Carla, I think you've got a dessert here that qualifies as a healthy serving of fruit."

1¼ cups flour

1 tablespoon baking powder

2 tablespoons sugar

1 teaspoon pumpkin pie spice

1 egg

1¼ cups buttermilk

Zest of ½ lemon

4 tablespoons butter, melted

2 medium Granny Smith apples, peeled and cored

1. Combine the dry ingredients and set aside. Whisk together the egg and buttermilk until smooth. Add the wet ingredients to the dry, and then fold in the lemon zest and stir in the butter. Cut the apples crosswise into ⅛-inch slices. Using a toothpick, dip the slices into the batter. Cook on a buttered griddle, over medium heat until golden brown, turning once. Serve hot with apple cider syrup.

APPLE CIDER SYRUP

MAKES 1 CUP | Cook time: 10 mins.

2 cups apple cider

Zest of ½ lemon

1 tablespoon cinnamon

½ cup brown sugar

In a small saucepan over medium heat add the apple cider and begin to reduce. Add the lemon zest, cinnamon, and brown sugar. Cook until liquid has reduced by half, about 10 minutes. Serve warm over batter fried apple rings.

CHEW CHEW CLUSTERS

SERVES 8 | **Skill Level: EASY** | **Cook Time: 10 mins.** | **Prep Time: 25 mins.** | **Cost: $**
Inactive Prep Time: 2–12 hrs.

If you have ever been to Nashville, Tennessee, you have probably come across a treat known as the GooGoo Cluster. It's kind of our official candy bar, a combination of chocolate, marshmallow fluff, caramel, and salted peanuts. Nashvillians revere it as the first combination chocolate and candy bar. This recipe is my made-from-scratch homage to the original. One of my big changes is to use dark chocolate, the best I can find. If you are not a peanut fancier, pecans work, as do walnuts or pine nuts. Basically, if it's a nut, go ahead and use it.

2 cups dark chocolate chips, melted

1 cup salted peanuts

1 cup caramel sauce (recipe follows)

17-ounce jar marshmallow cream

1. Place a teaspoon of melted dark chocolate in the bottom of a muffin tin. Then add a teaspoon of peanuts, a teaspoon of caramel sauce, and a teaspoon of marshmallow. Top with another teaspoon of the dark chocolate. Place in the fridge to firm up, about 2 hours and up to overnight.

CARAMEL SAUCE

1 cup sugar

½ cup heavy whipping cream

6 tablespoons butter

Heat the sugar on medium-high in a heavy-bottomed 3-quart sauce pot. As the sugar begins to brown, begin to whisk vigorously. Stop whisking as soon as the sugar is a golden amber color. In a slow stream, add the cream and whisk until the sauce is smooth. It will foam considerably during this step and the next. Remove from heat and add the butter, and whisk until the butter is incorporated. Allow the sauce to cool to room temperature before using.

TEN-GALLON APPLE PIE

SERVES 8 TO 10 | Skill Level: EASY | Cook Time: 30–40 mins. | Prep Time: 20 mins. | Cost: $

Inactive Prep Time: 1 hr.

Remember how in old cowboy movies they used to wear ten-gallon hats? They weren't really ten gallons, but the point was they were big. My Ten-Gallon Apple Pie is big in the same way. It takes more than 5 pounds of apples, and it's the most ginormous apple pie I have ever seen. It really makes an impression when you bring it to the table. And the aroma is pure heaven on a plate. It's not a hard pie to make if you cook down the apples first. That way they don't pile up so high that they won't fit in the crust.

FOR THE CRUST:

⅔ cup water

2 teaspoons salt

2 tablespoons sugar

4 cups all-purpose flour

4 sticks butter, chilled and cut into ½-inch cubes

FOR THE FILLING:

10 tablespoons unsalted butter

5¼ pounds Granny Smith apples, cored and sliced ⅛ inch thick

1¼ pounds empire or Fuji apples, cored and sliced ⅛ inch thick

2 cups sugar

2 teaspoons cinnamon

5 tablespoons bourbon or brandy

Juice of ½ lemon

1 teaspoon vanilla extract

TO FINISH:

Whites of 1 egg

1 tablespoon granulated sugar

TO MAKE THE CRUST:

1. Preheat the oven to 375 °F. Combine the water, salt, and sugar in a measuring cup. Stir and place the cup in the fridge for at least 15 minutes to chill. If possible, chill the mixing bowl and paddle attachment.

2. Combine the flour and butter pieces in the mixing bowl. On medium speed, cut the butter into the flour until the butter pieces are the size of small pebbles. With the mixer running, pour the water mixture into the flour-butter mixture. Mix until the dough comes together. Separate the dough into 2 discs. Wrap each with film and chill for at least 1 hour.

3. Roll 1 chilled pastry disc out to fit a deep-dish pie dish. Prick the dough all over with a fork. Bake 10–15 minutes, or until lightly golden. Set aside to cool.

Cooking by heart

It's very important that you taste your apples before you cook them and also after you cook them so you can be sure they have the right amount of sweetness. This is an example of "cooking by heart." That doesn't mean that you have memorized every recipe, but, instead, that you use your heart (and your taste buds) as you work through the recipe. Remember, any recipe is only a guide, and every ingredient is always a little different. Taste your food while you work. I do.

TO MAKE THE FILLING:

4. In a very large skillet, melt the butter over medium-high heat, then add the apples, sugar, and cinnamon. When the apples begin to sizzle, cover and reduce to a simmer. Cook, stirring occasionally, until the apples soften and release their juices, about 10–12 minutes. Add the bourbon or brandy, cook for another minute, then stir in the lemon juice and vanilla extract, and allow to cool. If needed, cook in batches and lay the filling out on a sheet to cool.

TO MAKE THE PIE:

5. Turn the oven down to 350 °F.

6. Roll out the remaining chilled piece of piecrust large enough to cover the pie.

7. Pour the filling into par-baked crust, and cover with the second piece of piecrust. Trim the cover, and fold under the edges. Flute the edges together or use a fork to press them together. Brush the top with egg whites and sprinkle with granulated sugar. Cut four slits near the center of the pie to vent steam. Bake for 25–30 minutes, until the crust is golden brown. Allow to cool before serving.

FALL

BLT BLOODY MARY

SERVES 1 | **Skill Level: EASY** | **Prep Time: 1–5 mins.** | **Cost: $**

My all-time favorite sandwich is a BLT, so I asked myself, how could you go wrong making it into a cocktail? Answer: you can't! Especially if you add some firepower with a blast of horseradish and for an exotic modern touch, coriander-infused vodka. Lotsa vodka!

FOR THE CORIANDER VODKA:

2 cups vodka

1 tablespoon coriander

FOR THE BLT BLOODY MARY:

2 ounces coriander vodka

4 ounces tomato juice

½ ounce lemon juice

¼ teaspoon hot pepper sauce

¼ teaspoon Worcestershire sauce

½ teaspoon bottled horseradish

Bacon, lettuce, and olive, for garnish

TO MAKE THE CORIANDER VODKA:

1. Combine the coriander and vodka and refrigerate overnight.

TO MAKE THE BLT BLOODY MARY:

2. Fill a cocktail shaker three-quarters full with ice. Add all the ingredients except the bacon, lettuce, and olive garnish, cover, and shake well. Strain into a highball glass filled with fresh ice. Garnish with skewer threaded with bacon, lettuce, and olive.

Clinton and Stacy London enjoying their perfectly blended cocktail.

THE STINTON

SERVES 1 | **Skill Level: EASY** | **Prep Time: 10 mins.** | **Cost: $**

Stacy London is my fabulous fashionista, sartorial sister, and cohost on What Not to Wear. *For those of you who think we sit around in our superstar trailer and drink gorgeous cocktails all day, I'm here to tell you that you're right.*

I wish.

Sometimes, though, we dream about what it would be like to kick back like old-time Hollywood stars and dive into a delicious cocktail. So when Stacy showed up on The Chew, *we got to live our dream—at least the cocktail-making part—and invented the Stinton, as in Stacy + Clinton = Stinton. Devilishly clever, don't you think? So add as much bourbon as you dare, cut it with some bitters, sweeten with some vermouth and a Maraschino cherry, and pretend you're Virginia Mayo.*

2 ounces bourbon

½ ounce sweet vermouth

2 dashes bitters

2 ounces seltzer

Maraschino cherry, for garnish

1. Combine the bourbon, vermouth, and bitters in a cocktail shaker. Shake well, strain into an old-fashioned glass, and top with a splash of seltzer. Garnish with a maraschino cherry.

POMEGRANATE SUNSET

| SERVES 1 | Skill Level: EASY | Cook Time: 15 mins. | Prep Time: 5 mins. | Cost: $ |

I like to have a signature cocktail for every season. From Memorial Day to Labor Day, I'm a gin-and-tonic man. From Labor Day to Memorial Day, a Manhattan is my choice. One day, after a couple of drinks, it dawned on me that the Manhattan was getting the better of that arrangement, so I decided to invent something for fall.

Hmm . . . what could it be?

I thought about Daphne, and when I think about Daphne, the second thing that I think about is antioxidants (the first is I love her to pieces). And then it came to me: pomegranates are in season in the fall and they are full of antioxidants. And thus, with the assistance of a bottle of vodka, orange juice, seltzer, and mint, the Pomegranate Sunset was born.

I suppose you could get the same amount of antioxidants without the vodka, but it wouldn't be as much fun.

FOR THE POMEGRANATE SYRUP:

1 cup sugar

1 cup pomegranate juice

FOR THE POMEGRANATE SUNSET:

2 ounces vodka

2 ounces orange juice

2 ounces seltzer

1 tablespoon pomegranate syrup (recipe follows)

Mint, for garnish

TO MAKE THE POMEGRANATE SYRUP

1. Pour one part pomegranate juice to one part sugar in a small saucepan. Simmer, stirring occasionally, until it thickens, about 15 minutes. Cool and refrigerate.

TO MAKE THE POMEGRANATE SUNSET

2. Mix vodka, orange juice, and seltzer. Add pomegranate syrup. Garnish with mint.

FALL

CRANBERRY SODA

SERVES 1 | Skill Level: EASY | Cook Time: 25 mins. | Prep Time: 15 mins. | Cost: $

Inactive Prep Time: 2 – 12 hrs.

I love tartness, the really good pucker that you get from lemons, limes, rhubarb, and cranberries. Since I am not an alcohol drinker, I came up with a signature "mocktail" for my catering business. Tart cranberry, floral spicy ginger, bitter fruity cranberries in simple syrup, and ripe sweet strawberries are a killer combination. Make this for the nondrinkers in your crowd. Drinkers, feel free to add your favorite clear booze.

FOR THE GINGER SIMPLE SYRUP:

¾ cup ginger, grated

2 cups granulated sugar, plus more for coating the cranberries

1½ cups water

1 cup whole cranberries, plus extra for garnish

FOR THE CRANBERRY SODA:

2 ounces ginger simple syrup

2 ounces cranberry juice (optional)

Juice of 1 lime

2 ounces sparkling water

TO MAKE THE GINGER SIMPLE SYRUP:

1. Place the ginger, sugar, and water in a small pot.

2. Place on medium heat and simmer until the sugar dissolves, about 10 minutes, and add the cranberries.

3. Remove from the heat and let steep for 15 minutes. Strain out the cranberries and cool completely. The syrup will be slightly pink.

4. Roll the cranberries in sugar. Lay them in a single layer on a sheet pan and freeze for about 2 hours and up to overnight.

TO MAKE THE CRANBERRY SODA:

5. Combine all the ingredients and garnish with 4–5 cranberries. Serve over ice.

WINTER

WARRIOR SALAD, 70 | WINTER GREEN SALAD WITH PEARS, AGED CHEDDAR, AND ALMONDS, 71 | BRAISED PORK SHANKS, 72 | WHITE BEANS, PORK, AND COLLARD GREENS SOUP, 74 | CHILAQUILES, 79 | EGGS IN HELL, 80 | EGGS IN HEAVEN, 82 | SLOW COOKER PEACHY CHICKEN, 83 | GRILLED CHICKEN AND FENNEL SALAD, 84 | PORK AU POIVRE, 87 | CHAMPAGNE CROWN ROAST, 89 | HOLIDAY MAC 'N' CHEESE CASSEROLE, 90 | MICHAEL'S CHICKEN CHILI, 94 | MARIO'S RESTRICTOR PLATE CHILI, 95 | CHILI CON CARLA, 97 | DAPHNE'S VEGGIE CHILI, 99 | DEEP-DISH PIZZA CASSEROLE, 100 | MEATLOAF ALLA MARIO, 103 | CHOCAHOLIC WHOOPIE PIES, 105 | GRILLED BACON, CHOCOLATE-HAZELNUT SANDWICH, 108 | HOT MUTTERED BUM, 112 | ROLES ROYCE, 113 | POTATO LEEK SOUP, 114 | IRISH SODA BREAD, 116 | SUPER BOWL PUNCH, 118 | THE WARM AND TOASTY, 119 | SPICY GRAPEFRUIT MARGARITA, AKA "THE CLINTON CALIENTE," 120

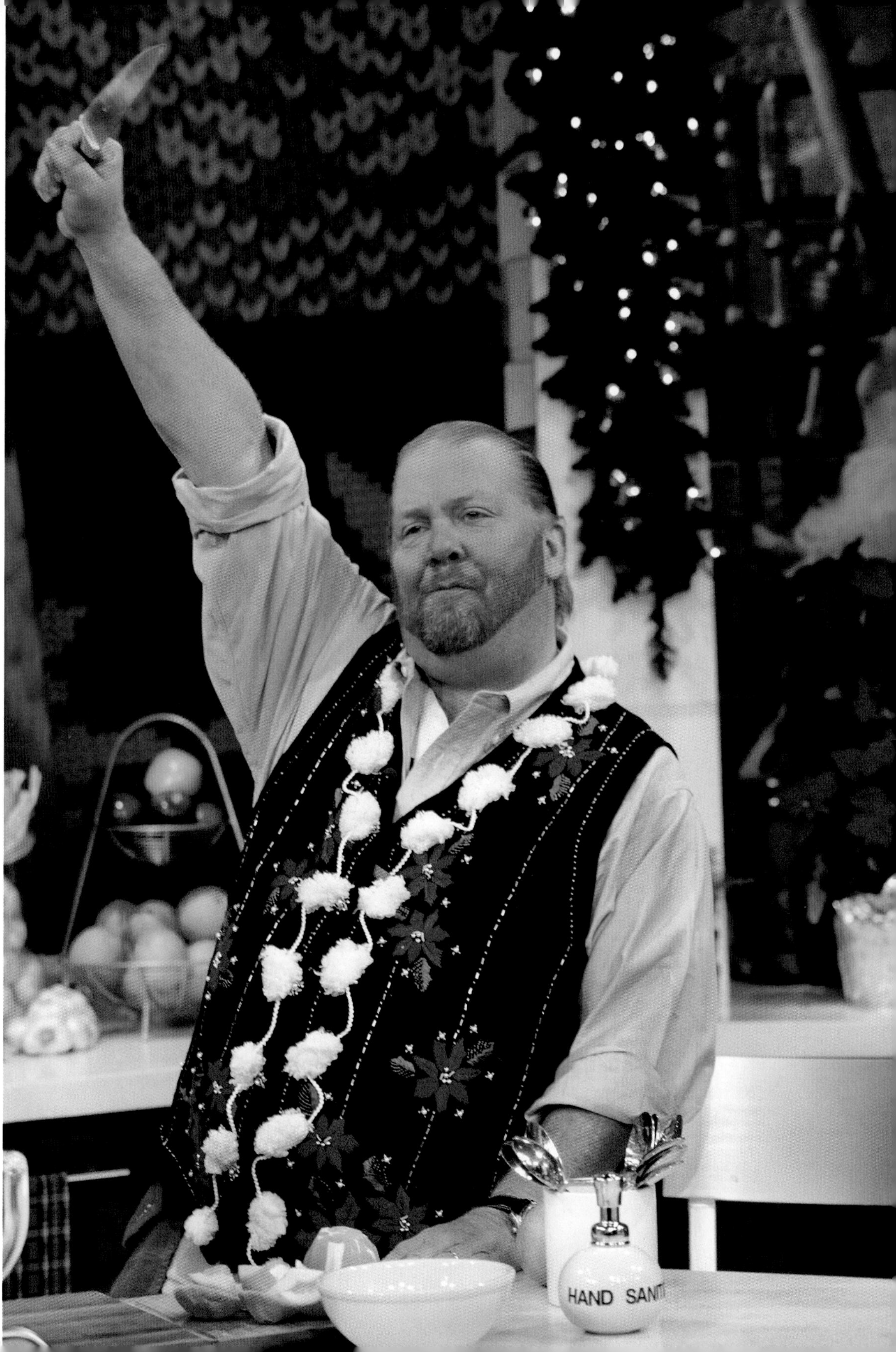

Q&A

Mario

Q: **You've done a lot of cooking on TV. How is *The Chew* different? How do you like being on the show?**

Mario: Well, the first thing I must say is that I probably never would have met these people had we not been put together in this show. Everyone is really nice; no one has any ulterior motives other than the show's success and speaking their own mind—whether it's food or fashion or crafts or whatever. The format is very easy to come into every morning—they hand us notes the night before. Whether you read them or not, you will not be quizzed or tested. If you want to sound smart, you can; if you want to sound silly or goofy, you can. And there're no rules, so we can't possibly break them. It's a very refreshing and relaxing format that allows us to chitchat, so we feel a lot more like we do in our kitchens, as opposed to some giant studio, and in the relaxing moments when it's really gelling and everyone's cooking and really digging what everyone else does—it's very informative, without being like a talking textbook.

WINTER

67

Q: *The Chew* is like one big dinner party, with everyone gathering in the kitchen. The food is so relaxed and accessible. Is it different from the fancier kitchens you're used to?

Mario: Our kitchen is our living room, so when people are at our house for dinner, I'm in the kitchen just like this, so it doesn't look very much different at all from my daily experience in my house. *The Chew* appeals to people who are comfortable in the kitchen. They just need some new ideas. Many of them have basically rounded their wagon around a campfire of ten or fifteen dishes that they make slight variations on all the time. And seeing new kinds of food presented in a less-than-fifteen-minutes kind of real cooking time empowers and inspires them to look at ingredients in a different way. Our goal is "Let's help people get in the kitchen; let's remove the obstacles from them and just inspire people to be happy in their kitchens, to create delicious and healthy food without being heavy-handed or 'this is the only way.'" It's just, "Look, this is quick. This is easy. This is how we like to do it. Don't overthink it, but make something delicious work."

Q: **When Michael does his 5-in-5s, he'll sometimes stop to do little asides in the middle of it. And you'll say, just like on *Iron Chef*, "Uh, 2 minutes and 43 seconds, Chef." And he's just as cool as can be. Do you ever worry that he won't make it?**

Mario: He slows down on purpose because he knows he's going to get there. And that, to his credit, is probably why he is one of the most top-winning Iron Chefs. And also why he's a compelling instructor. Because for him, there is no rush. You're just going to get it done—just stay on it.

Q: **You did a series in Spain with Gwyneth Paltrow and Mark Bittman. Spanish cooking is so influential in the world today. Would you like to bring that, or any other global influences, to *The Chew*?**

Mario: I think the Iberian Peninsula and Portuguese food isn't really hot yet with the cooking public, but it's going to be pretty soon. I love their kind of fantasy Catalan mind-set that people like Salvador Dalí and Picasso and Miró brought to painting. They have always lived on the vanguard.

I don't think we'll create balls of olive oil juice here, but we're definitely going to cook certain traditional Spanish food or even more thought-provoking modern Spanish food. But basically, *The Chew* is going to be about cooking at home; that's the story. As weird as the stuff is that I bring back, I still want it to reference what people can actually do in their home.

WARRIOR SALAD

SERVES 4 | **Skill Level: EASY** | **Cook Time: 15 mins.** | **Prep Time: 10 mins.** | **Cost: $**

Everybody has—or at least should have—some ingredients on hand that they can toss together for a quick and delicious meal. I always have some cooked quinoa in my fridge. Quinoa is very high in protein. For the same reason, I also have a few kinds of beans on hand. These ingredients are like flavor sponges. They pick up the flavors of whatever you combine them with. I looked over the shelves to see what other ingredients I could gather together. Mustard, maple syrup, olive oil, and dried cranberries all called out to me. I imagined the flavors my mom would combine and this is the result. I call it Warrior Salad because it's full of protein and complex carbs and low in fat: just the thing for a warrior going into battle, or an average American just returned from a day of corporate combat and looking for something quick and healthy for dinner.

FOR THE DRESSING:

3 tablespoons extra virgin olive oil

Juice of ½ lemon

½ teaspoon maple syrup

1 teaspoon whole grain mustard

Salt, to taste

Pepper, to taste

FOR THE SALAD:

2 cups cooked quinoa, cooked to package instructions

¾ cup chickpeas, drained and rinsed

¼ cup dried cranberries

¼ cup scallions, thinly sliced

1. For the dressing, combine the olive oil, lemon juice, maple syrup, and mustard. Season with salt and pepper to taste. Stir well. Combine all the remaining ingredients in a bowl, and toss with the dressing.

Quinoa quick fact

Quinoa is one of the many gifts of the New World to the food world. A thousand years ago, the Incas cultivated it as a source of protein and complex carbs (the good kind). It is very easy to cook: just add liquid and salt and simmer. It will keep in the fridge for days and goes well in soups and salads or reheated with some sautéed onions and served on the side like mashed potatoes.

WINTER GREEN SALAD WITH PEARS, AGED CHEDDAR, AND ALMONDS

SERVES 6 | Skill Level: EASY | Prep Time: 20 mins. | Cost: $

Summer salads make me think of light tastes and textures. A winter salad, like winter food, wants to be assertive. It needs to pull you by the palate and say, "Hey, you're gonna pay attention." I made this salad with pears from the green market and some local Cheddar. Watercress adds crunchiness, and so do the almonds. Serve it with roasted chicken and your chicken will say, "Thank you."

4 medium heads Belgian endive

2 medium shallots, finely diced

1 tablespoon red wine vinegar

Salt

2 tablespoons extra virgin olive oil

Freshly ground black pepper

1 bunch watercress, thick stems trimmed, cut into 3-inch sprigs

1 large pear, thinly sliced

1 tablespoon chives, cut at an angle into ¼-inch lengths

1 tablespoon flat-leaf parsley, coarsely chopped

⅓ cup almonds, toasted and coarsely chopped

¼ cup aged NY Cheddar cheese, crumbled

1. Remove the outer leaves of the endives and cut in half lengthwise. Cut into 1-inch-thick slices on the bias. Set aside.

2. Next, mix the shallots, vinegar, and salt in a bowl. Set aside for 5 minutes to allow the flavors to marry. Whisk the olive oil into the vinegar mixture and season with pepper. Taste and adjust seasoning.

3. Combine the endives, watercress, pear, chives, parsley, and vinaigrette in a large bowl and toss to coat. Arrange on a platter, and top with the almonds and cheese.

BRAISED PORK SHANKS

| SERVES 4 with leftovers | Skill Level: MODERATE | Cook Time: 4–5 hrs. | Cost: $$ |

Prep Time: 15 mins. | Inactive Prep time: 12 hrs.

This is a super succulent, deeply flavored main course. With some mashed potatoes, parsnips, or polenta, it is a great winter meal to have after a snow-shoveling session. We made this on the show as one of our two-fer segments: how to get more than one meal out of a recipe. You can make the recipe with any braised meat, but on The Chew *I did it with pork. But before we get to that second meal, first you have to make your braise for your first meal.*

FOR THE BRINE:

1 gallon water

1 cup kosher salt

½ cup sugar

1 head garlic, halved

2 sprigs fresh rosemary

1 tablespoon black peppercorns

1 tablespoon coriander

1 bay leaf

6 pork shanks

FOR THE BRAISE:

Canola oil

Flour, for dredging

3 cups celery, roughly chopped

2 cups carrots, roughly chopped

1 Spanish onion, chopped

3 cloves garlic, smashed

Large pinch of salt

1 sprig rosemary

1 small bundle of thyme

2 cups white wine

2 cups apple cider

4 quarts chicken stock

1. In a large nonreactive pot, combine all the brine ingredients and bring to a simmer. Whisk until the salt and sugar are completely dissolved. Remove from heat and let cool. In a container large enough to hold the shanks, completely submerge them in the cooled brine. Weigh down the shanks with a heavy plate, if necessary, to keep them fully submerged. Refrigerate overnight.

2. The next day, preheat the oven to 300 °F.

3. Remove the shanks from the brine, discarding the liquid. Heat a large Dutch oven over medium-high heat. Pour in enough canola oil to completely coat the bottom of the pot. Dredge the shanks in flour, shaking off any excess. In batches, begin browning the shanks, cooking a few minutes on each side. When browned, transfer the shanks to a plate, and begin browning the next batch.

4. Pour off all but 2 or 3 tablespoons of fat from the pot. Add the celery, carrots, onion, and garlic cloves, along with a large pinch of salt. Cook the vegetables until tender, about 7 minutes. Add the rosemary and thyme, and cook for another minute. Deglaze the pot with the white wine, and reduce by three-quarters. Add the apple cider and reduce by half. Add the chicken stock and bring the braising liquid up to a simmer. Taste and adjust for seasoning.

5. Return the shanks to the pot, cover, and place in the oven until the meat is tender, about 4–5 hours. Strain the braising liquid and serve with the shanks. Store any leftovers in their liquid. Refrigerate.

6. Use any remaining pork to make White Beans, Pork, and Collard Greens Soup (see page 74).

Michael and Rachael Ray whip up some trouble.

WHITE BEANS, PORK, AND COLLARD GREENS SOUP

SERVES 8 | Skill Level: EASY | Cook Time: 45 mins. | Prep Time: 20 mins. | Cost: $

Comfort food is just another way of saying, "I like this, it makes me kind of smile, and it doesn't take a lot of fussing to throw together." This bowl of heartwarming comfort fits the bill. It's really one of my favorite stay-at-home wintry meals. Even though winter has its challenges, I kind of hope our recent warm winters aren't a trend. I like an occasional midwestern cold snap, battening down the hatches, hanging around the fire, and smelling the house fill up with aromas on a winter afternoon.

Leftover Braised Pork Shanks, shredded (see page 72)

¼ cup olive oil

2½ cups onion, diced small

Salt

½ pound sweet Italian sausage, casings removed and filling broken up

1 teaspoon chili flakes

2 cups low-sodium chicken stock

½ pound (1 cup) dried navy beans or great northern beans, soaked

1 bay leaf

1 15.5-ounce can cannellini beans

8 cups collard greens leaves, washed and roughly chopped

Pepper

Pecorino Romano, grated, for garnish

1. Place a soup pot over medium-high heat and add the olive oil. When the oil is hot, add the onions with a large pinch of salt. Cook the onions until they start to soften, about 3 minutes.

2. Next add the sausage, breaking it up into smaller pieces as you add it to the pot. When the sausage starts to brown, add the chili flakes, and cook for another minute.

3. Add the chicken stock, navy or great northern beans, and bay leaf, and bring the liquid up to a gentle boil. After the soup comes up to a boil, reduce it to a simmer and cook for an hour on medium-low heat, stirring occasionally.

4. After an hour, add the can of cannellini beans with their liquid. Bring to a simmer.

5. Add all the collard greens to the pot with a little more salt and pepper. Cook for another 30 minutes. Stir in the shredded pork and cook just to warm through.

6. To serve, ladle the soup into bowls, and grate a good amount of cheese over the top.

There is no such thing as a quick collard

Collard greens want to be cooked for a good long while. They are one of the few greens that actually improve from long cooking. In the wintertime, they are also one of the only local, fresh green leafy vegetables available. Apart from being good for you, they give you the chance to say, "I'm making a mess o' greens."

'Tis the Season for Parties

THERE ARE A MILLION THINGS to think about when you are hosting a get-together. Since I host a lot of parties, I thought I'd share some of my favorite home entertaining tips (and one cool trick).

Lighting

The best thing you can to do is invest in an electrician. Every light in your house should always be on a dimmer. Why? Because everyone looks better in dim light. You do not want overhead lighting at your party. It's very harsh. If you can't afford an electrician right now, get yourself a whole bunch of candles, because candles make everybody look good.

Can(dle) do

Keep candles about 9 inches away from the edge of anything that you are putting them on, because I found out once the hard way with a friend who was wearing an angora sweater. That thing went right up. So keep them 9 inches away from the edge. Never put candles between people and anything they might want to reach for, like food or drink. And no scented candles near the food! However, do put a scented candle in the bathroom, because, well . . . you know why.

Napkin notes

If I'm having a big party, I use paper napkins. But if you want to be environmentally correct (I sure do), then if I'm having a smaller party, I put out cloth napkins. Washcloths—four for a dollar—work as napkins or hand towels. If you have a restaurant supply store nearby, you can sometimes buy cloth napkins cheaply and in bulk. Tie each napkin or towel in a ribbon or a little bit of raffia.

Don't forget the hamper

People will need someplace to discard used napkins. Put a sign up: DIRTY NAPKINS GO HERE. And while you're at it, put a hamper right under that sign. Ditto for used hand towels in the bathroom.

Ice is nice

If you do not have enough ice at the party, you will kill it. That's the worst thing, because when latecomers show up, all you'll have to offer is room temperature rum and Coke. That's not fun. Get enough ice: 1 pound per person for most of the year, but I bump it to 2 pounds in summer.

Also, remember, ice melts, and no one likes to slosh around a cold puddle with a pair of tongs. Put ice cubes in a colander or strainer over a bowl. That way, the ice melt drips into the bowl and the cubes stay relatively dryish.

Trash tips

Have you ever woken up after a party and found a bunch of olive pits in your potted plants? I once found shrimp tails in my bedroom and watermelon pits in a bowling trophy. Make sure you leave out some bowls for discards and, just like with the towels and napkins, put up a sign so people know what to do.

Marbles. yes, marbles.

Put some marbles in your medicine cabinet before the party starts. The first person to go snooping for drugs is in for a surprise. When the marbles fall on the floor, you'll hear the *ping ping, ping* over the loudest Jay-Z track. You'll also learn something about your friends in the process.

Do yourself a favor

Everyone likes a gift. I always put a big bowl of something special at the door. Sometimes I make peanut brittle and put it in little bags. Or brownies, or wine charms. It doesn't have to be much. It really is the thought that counts: one last nice thing you can do as host that your guests can enjoy after they have gone home, and you have cleaned the kitchen . . . and collapsed.

The Rockettes get a kick out of *The Chew* crew.

Stay smooth

The key to making nice, smooth scrambled eggs is to whisk them as they cook. The chef's term is an *even curd*, which means ultrasmooth and creamy. Also, you could use store-bought tortilla chips for this, but you will get a wonderful mix of chewy and crispy if you start with fresh tortillas and crisp them yourself.

CHILAQUILES

SERVES 4 | **Skill Level: EASY** | **Cook Time: 5 mins.** | **Prep Time: 10 mins.** | **Cost: $**

I made this on President's Day when we all dressed up as our favorite president. I picked Benjamin Franklin. Yeah, yeah, I know, he wasn't a president, but he is on the hundred-dollar bill, which will get you a lot further in New York than being a member of the Herbert Hoover Fan Club. I chose a very American dish—by that I mean something we owe to our immigrant heritage. In this case, the heritage is Mexican-American: chilaquiles, otherwise known as fried tortilla chips, eggs, cheese, and spiciness. I'm told that President Obama loves this for breakfast. When I made this on the show, Michael said whenever they ask me how long a recipe takes I always say 2 minutes. Guess what? This one actually took me 2 minutes!

4 tablespoons extra virgin olive oil

6 blue corn tortillas

1 tablespoon kosher salt

4 tablespoons unsalted butter

6 eggs, lightly beaten

2 cups store-bought roasted tomatillo salsa

1½ cups white Cheddar cheese, grated, to serve

½ cup sour cream, to serve

¼ cup fresh cilantro leaves, chopped, to garnish

2 limes, cut into wedges, to garnish

1. Heat the olive oil in a 10-inch nonstick pan over medium-high heat. Cut the tortillas into 8 pieces each, like a pie. Carefully add the tortillas to the hot oil and cook until crisp, about 3–4 minutes, stirring constantly. Remove pieces to a paper towel to drain and sprinkle with a little salt.

2. Pour out any excess oil from the pan and reduce heat to medium. Add the butter to the pan and swirl until light golden brown. Add the eggs and the tomatillo salsa, season with salt and pepper, and cook slowly, stirring constantly with a whisk, until soft curds form. Add the cooked tortillas and half of the cheese, and stir through until just set.

3. To serve, place some of the eggs on each plate and top with some Cheddar cheese and a dollop of the sour cream. Garnish each serving with a tablespoon of the chopped cilantro leaves and a lime wedge.

EGGS IN HELL

SERVES 4 | Skill Level: EASY | Cook Time: 20 mins. | Prep Time: 5 mins. | Cost: $

If you can poach an egg, sauté vegetables, and throw some tomatoes in a skillet, you already know all the cooking techniques you need to make this dish. It's nothing more than poached eggs in a spicy tomato sauce. How spicy? That's where the "hell" part comes in. I like mine molto spicy, as in I use fresh jalapeños with all of their fiery seeds. If you don't like yours so spicy, then cut back on the hot stuff. Maybe you could call it Eggs in Purgatory, then.

This is a perfect brunch recipe. I am major league into brunch, because it's a time when people actually chill. No one is on the clock. And in terms of value received for time spent, it takes the least amount of worry and rush, and with the proper amount of Bloody Marys or mimosas, you can linger over it all afternoon and follow it up with a well-deserved nap.

4 tablespoons extra virgin olive oil

1 medium onion, coarsely chopped

6 cloves garlic, thinly sliced

4 jalapeño peppers, cut into ¼-inch dice

1 teaspoon hot chili flakes

3 cups Mario's Basic Tomato Sauce (see page 30)

½ cup water

8 large eggs

¼ cup Parmigiano-Reggiano or Pecorino, grated

Salt

Pepper

¼ cup basil, shredded

1. Place a skillet over medium-high heat. Add the oil and heat until just smoking.

2. Add the chopped onion, garlic, jalapeños, and chili flakes, and cook until softened and light brown, about 7 minutes.

3. Add the tomato sauce and water and bring to a boil. Immediately lower the heat to a simmer and carefully crack the eggs, one by one, into the tomato sauce. Season with salt and pepper. Cover and cook until the whites set but the yolks are still quite runny, about 5–6 minutes.

4. Remove the pan from the heat and sprinkle with cheese and some shredded basil. Allow to cool, about 3–4 minutes. Garnish with basil and serve.

In praise of old black skillets

This is a dish for your trusty black skillet. And if you don't have a trusty black skillet, take this as your excuse to go get one. Among its many virtues—such as even heating—it also looks nice. You can cook and serve in it, which makes for one less platter to clean.

EGGS IN HEAVEN

SERVES 6 | Skill Level: EASY | Cook Time: 30–40 mins. | Prep Time: 10 mins. | Cost: $

Mario made Eggs in Hell, which inspired me to make Eggs in Heaven. If you're from the South, you can be forgiven for substituting the word grits for heaven. Rich, creamy grits are one of the simplest and most glorious foods, especially when made even richer and creamier with some melted cheese.

For some reason, grits have never caught on in the rest of the country like they have in Dixie. In fact, when I asked for a quick show of hands from our studio audience, there were only two members who admitted openly to grits eating.

This recipe will change your mind and it's totally simple. You make some grits, you add some cheese, and then you bake your eggs in them.

Very easy. Very delicious. So y'all get in the kitchen and start cooking.

1½ cups water

1 cup whole milk

1 teaspoon salt

1 cup stone-ground hominy grits or quick grits

4 tablespoons butter

½ cup Cheddar cheese, shredded

¼ cup parsley

Vegetable oil spray

6 eggs

Black pepper, to taste

1 ham steak, grilled, to serve

1. Preheat the oven to 350 °F.

2. In a 3-quart heavy-bottomed pot, bring water, milk, and salt to a boil. Gradually stir in the grits and reduce heat. Simmer for 20–25 minutes, or until thick. Whisk often to prevent lumps.

3. Stir in the butter and cheese. Pour the grits into an 11-by-7-inch glass baking dish.

4. Make 6 depressions in the grits mixture about 2 inches apart with the back of a spoon sprayed with oil spray. Carefully break one egg into each depression. Sprinkle with freshly ground black pepper.

5. Bake uncovered for 10–15 minutes, or until eggs are at desired doneness. Garnish with chopped parsley. Serve hot with a grilled ham steak.

Quick is good, too quick isn't

Depending on how your grits are milled, they can take up to 40 minutes to make. Quick grits often claim they can be ready in 5 minutes. As far as I am concerned, there is nothing quick about grits. They need a good 20 minutes cooking in half milk and half water, with some butter and salt at the end. That's the only way to get them good and creamy and thick. Soupy grits are just no fun.

SLOW COOKER PEACHY CHICKEN

SERVES 6 TO 8 | **Skill Level: EASY** | **Cook Time: 6–8 hrs.** | **Prep Time: 10 mins.** | **Cost: $**

If I had to pick my favorite type of cuisine, it would either be Mexican, Persian, or Moroccan food, because I love adding sweetness and spice to the same meal. It awakens the palate in a totally different way. This dish always makes me think of a Moroccan tagine, the way it mixes chicken, peaches, and even a little apricot jam, plus a whole lot of vegetables. You put all the fruits and veggies and seasonings in your slow cooker, then place the chicken on top with a little broth or apple cider. Turn on the cooker. Go to work. Come home at the end of the day, and you have this succulent, sweet, hot, aromatic chicken that has been slowly burbling and steaming all day. If you are looking for minimal work, minimal calories, and super high flavor, these kinds of slow cooker dishes fit the bill.

FOR THE CHICKEN:

8 boneless, skinless chicken thighs

Salt

Pepper

3 sweet potatoes, cut into 1-inch cubes

1 onion, diced

1 tablespoon low-sodium soy sauce

3 tablespoons apple cider vinegar

3 cups chicken stock

1 cup peach preserves

1 tablespoon ginger, freshly grated

1 teaspoon curry powder

1 teaspoon paprika

1 teaspoon cayenne pepper

FOR THE SPINACH:

2 tablespoons extra virgin olive oil

1 clove garlic, sliced

1 bunch baby spinach, washed and trimmed

Salt

1 teaspoon sesame seeds

TO MAKE THE CHICKEN:

1. Season the chicken with salt and pepper.

2. Put the cubed sweet potatoes and onions into the slow cooker and top with the seasoned chicken.

3. Mix together the soy sauce, apple cider vinegar, chicken stock, and peach preserves, then pour over the chicken.

4. Sprinkle the chicken with salt, ginger, curry powder, paprika, and cayenne pepper.

5. Cook on low for 6–8 hours, until chicken is cooked through and potatoes are fork-tender.

TO MAKE THE SPINACH:

6. Meanwhile, in a large nonstick skillet, add the olive oil and bring to medium heat. Add the garlic. Once the garlic is fragrant, add the spinach, season with salt, and cook until wilted. Fold in the sesame seeds and transfer to a platter. Serve with the chicken.

Less than you think

When you are translating one of your favorite recipes into a slow cooker version, remember it takes less liquid because no steam escapes and any fruits or vegetables will also give up their water. My rule of thumb is about a third less liquid.

GRILLED CHICKEN AND FENNEL SALAD

SERVES 6 | Skill Level: MODERATE | Cook Time: 15–30 mins. | Prep Time: 15 mins. | Cost: $$

One of my family's faves is this chicken, soaked in a super flavorful marinade and then grilled pressed down under a brick. My update is to use boneless dark meat, because it stays succulent and juicy and has better deliciousness. White meat is a more temperamental meat. Add to that the fact that this costs $3.50 per serving, and the check balancer in the family has got to like that.

As for fennel, fennel needs more cheerleaders in its corner. Fennel is almost like celery meets licorice in a magnificent marriage of delicious beauty. I love it, but if you don't then you can definitely substitute with Savoy cabbage or celery or green apple. The big point here is we have a grill dish and salad that you can make in the winter with fresh, crunchy vegetables. Never underestimate the joy of a fresh vegetable when it's slushy and snowy outside.

FOR THE TAPENADE:

6 anchovy fillets, soaked in milk overnight

2 tablespoons anchovy paste

1 cup pitted black olives

¼ cup capers, roughly chopped

3 tablespoons Dijon mustard

3 tablespoons red wine vinegar

5 tablespoons extra virgin olive oil

FOR THE SALAD:

½ bulb fennel, thinly sliced

Zest and segments of 1 orange

1 pound arugula leaves

3 tablespoons white or red wine vinegar

4 tablespoons extra virgin olive oil

Salt, to taste

Pepper, to taste

TO MAKE THE TAPENADE:

1. Combine all the ingredients in a food processor and blend until a smooth paste is formed, about 2 minutes. Transfer to a jar, cover tightly, and store in the refrigerator up to 6 weeks.

TO MAKE THE SALAD:

2. Mix all the ingredients together, and set aside.

TO MAKE THE CHICKEN:

3. In a large mixing bowl, mix ½ cup of tapenade and the olive oil, thyme, pepper, and red pepper flakes until well blended.

The marvelous afterlife of marinade

Once you have made a delicious marinade, don't toss it. If you put it on the grill pan, it bubbles and steams and infuses the chicken with beautiful flavor.

¾ cup olive oil

2 teaspoons fresh thyme leaves, chopped

2 teaspoons freshly ground black pepper

1 teaspoon red pepper flakes

6 boneless chicken thighs

SPECIAL EQUIPMENT:

Brick wrapped in foil

4. Add the chicken and toss to coat.

5. Place the chicken skin side down on the grill, 8–10 inches from the coals, and place a brick wrapped in foil on top. Cook slowly, about 6 minutes per side, until skin is crisp and brown and juices run clear when the chicken is pricked with a sharp knife at the thickest part of the thigh. Set aside and keep warm.

6. Place each chicken thigh over the fennel salad on each plate. Spoon 1 tablespoon tapenade over each half and serve immediately.

Tapenade is tops, anchovy is aces

This wonderful traditional mix of olives, anchovies, and herbs is a go-to flavor bomb and super all by itself on a crostini. Many people get a little finicky about anchovies. I'm here to tell you, please give them another try. They bring a mystical salinity, a backbone bass note to anything you cook them in. I tame mine a bit by soaking them in milk, which tones down the saltiness and does away with what I call the "pizzeria" anchovy flavor.

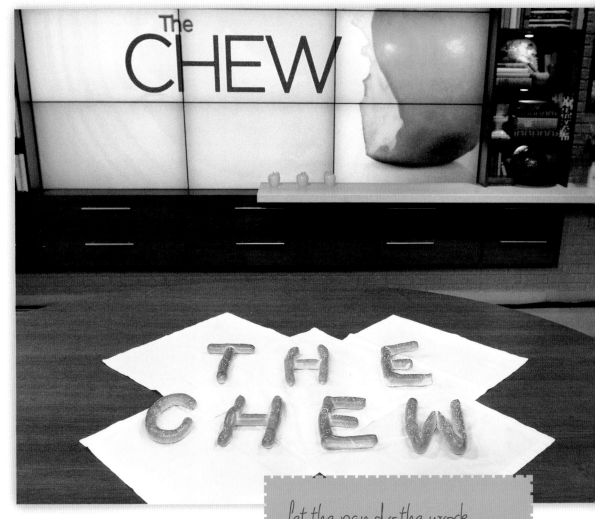

Let the pan do the work

If you watch enough cooking shows, you can be forgiven for thinking that the mark of a good chef is flipping things in pans as fast as you can. In fact, nothing could be further from the truth. As you can see in this recipe, I put the pork medallions in some oil and butter and leave them without moving. After they are about 75 percent cooked, I turn the meat and add liquid, which finishes the cooking with a gentle braise. That way you get a beautiful, full-flavored, crunchy crust and tender pork on the inside.

PORK AU POIVRE

SERVES 5 | **Skill Level: MODERATE** | **Cook Time: 10–15 mins.** | **Prep Time: 10 mins.** | **COST: $$**

I loved the movie Midnight in Paris. *Why? Two reasons: I love Woody Allen and I love Paris. So in honor of it winning an Oscar, we made this French bistro classic. All that was missing on the set of* The Chew *was a guy wearing a beret with a cigarette hanging out of his mouth. Michael was originally cast for the role, but then he went and quit smoking on us. It's a very basic bistro dish—the combination of pork, peppercorns, apples, apple brandy (calvados), and—mais oui—butter. I can't guarantee Hemingway and Toulouse-Lautrec will show up at your dinner party, like they did in the movie, but it's worth a try. As someone must have said in apple brandy country, "With enough calvados, anything is possible."*

1 pork tenderloin, cut into 5 medallions

Salt and freshly cracked black pepper

Flour, for dredging

2 tablespoons olive oil, divided

6 tablespoons butter

2 tablespoons green peppercorns

1 tablespoon whole grain mustard

½ cup apple brandy, divided

3 tablespoons crème fraîche

3 Granny Smith apples, sliced

½ cup chicken stock

2 tablespoons chives, chopped

1. Lightly pound each of the pork medallions and season on both sides with salt and pepper. Dredge each medallion in flour.

2. Heat a sauté pan over medium-high heat. Add 1 table-spoon olive oil and 2 tablespoons butter to pan. Add pork medallions and sear about 2 minutes per side. Add the green peppercorns, grainy mustard, and ¼ cup of the brandy. Cook for about 3 minutes. Flip the medallions and add crème fraîche, stirring into the juices to begin making the sauce. Cook for another 1–2 minutes.

3. Meanwhile, in a separate sauté pan over medium-high heat add remaining tablespoon of olive oil and 2 tablespoons of butter. Add sliced apples and cook for 1–2 minutes. Deglaze pan with remaining ¼ cup of brandy. If desired you can flambé the apples by igniting the brandy with a far-reaching flame. Add chicken stock, remaining butter, and salt to taste. Cook for another 2–3 minutes until apples are slightly softened.

4. To serve, plate some of the apple mixture and top with one of the medallions and some of the sauce. Garnish with chopped chives and serve.

WINTER

87

The Champagne gambit

A real visual crowd pleaser is to bring the pork—with the crown still intact—to the table and, while it is still hot, place a semi-chilled bottle of Champagne in the center. Carefully pop the cork and watch the contents overflow in a fountain of Champagne suds that bathes the pork and mixes in the cabbage braise. A word of caution here: This usually works and impresses people no end. But sometimes (like when I tried it on *The Chew* in front of millions of viewers) nothing happens when I pop the cork. At that point, you just say, "Oh well . . . ," pick up the bottle, and pour Champagne over the pork. It's still delightful to watch, and the fact that you are not bummered usually gets a round of cheers from the folks at your table.

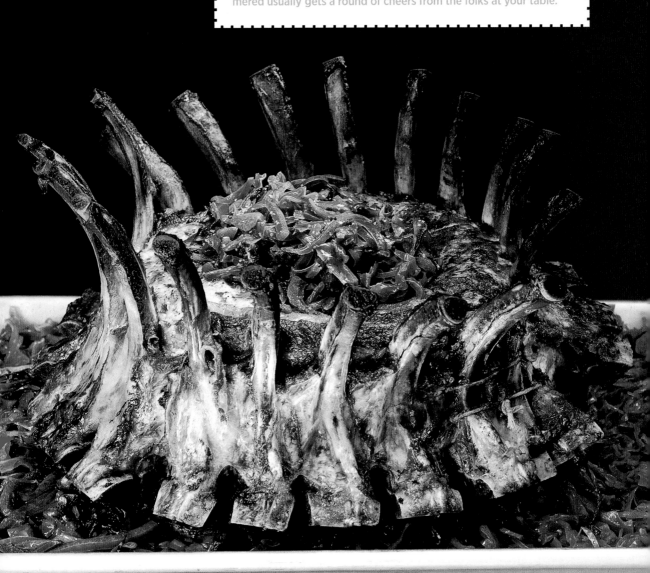

CHAMPAGNE CROWN ROAST

SERVES 10 | **Skill Level: MODERATE** | **Cook Time: 45 mins. – 1 hr.** | **Prep Time: 20 mins.**

Cost: $$ | **Inactive Prep time: 12 hrs.**

This is a "No Doubt about It" recipe, as in, it looks so dramatic when you bring it to the table that there is no doubt that this is a meal to serve on special festive occasions. In our house, that occasion is New Year's. Hogs are supposed to bring good luck, and this is about 6 pounds of good luck on a platter. Made on a bed of braised cabbage, with spices, oranges (plus zest, plus juice), and some chili peppers for zing, and finished with Champagne—it is one of my favorite meals.

1 6-pound bone-in pork loin roast

Kosher salt, to taste

Freshly ground black pepper, to taste

2 tablespoons olive oil

1 red cabbage, cored and sliced

3 red onions, sliced

2 Fresno chilies, thinly sliced into rounds

2 tablespoons caraway seeds, toasted

1 New Mexican chili, toasted to release oils

2 cups chicken stock, hot

Juice of 4 oranges, plus zest of ½ orange

2 tablespoons whole grain mustard

Splash sherry vinegar

1 bottle Champagne (semi-chilled)

½ bunch fresh cilantro, leaves picked, for garnish

1. Preheat the oven to 375 °F.

2. Generously season the pork all over with kosher salt and freshly ground black pepper. If possible, let it sit in the refrigerator overnight and bring to room temperature prior to cooking.

3. In a large roasting pan, add the olive oil and heat over medium heat. Add the cabbage, onions, Fresnos, toasted caraway seeds, New Mexican chili, salt, chicken stock, and orange juice. Top the vegetables with the pork roast.

4. Leave uncovered and place into the oven for about 45 minutes to 1 hour, or until the internal temperature on an instant-read thermometer reads between 140–145 °F.

5. When ready, remove the pork from the oven and place onto the stovetop or heatproof surface. Remove the pork from the pan and set aside. Add mustard, orange zest, and vinegar to the cabbage mixture, and stir to combine. Taste and season with salt. Return the pork to the pan. Lean the pork against the side of the pan. Place the semi-chilled Champagne bottle into the pan and take the cage off the top. You can let the top pop on its own or loosen it slowly with a kitchen towel. Allow some of the Champagne, about 2 cups, to spill into the pan.

6. Remove the pork from the pan and allow it to rest briefly on a cutting board. Remove the pork loin from the bone and slice. Place the cabbage onto a family-style platter. Fan the pork slices around the cabbage. Carve between the bones and add the bones to the platter. Garnish with cilantro leaves and spoon the pan sauce around the pork.

HOLIDAY MAC 'N' CHEESE CASSEROLE

| SERVES 8 | Skill Level: EASY | Cook Time: 30 mins. | Prep Time: 15 mins. | Cost: $ |

One of the great joys of being a parent is reconnecting with mac 'n' cheese. If you have been away from it for a few years, I guarantee that as soon as the kids are ready to eat solid food, mac 'n' cheese becomes a go-to kid pleaser. Pretty soon, you'll find yourself making a little extra and then, when your child doesn't finish the whole serving, grabbing a spoon and polishing it off, straight from the casserole dish.

My approach to mac 'n' cheese reflects my belief in what I call the "Go Big or Go Home Theory." I want a good mix of cheese and lots of it. Gruyère is terrific because it has a slight sharp bite, some aged stinkiness, and I swear a little bit of happiness in it. Must be the contented cows. And then there's creamy, sweet mascarpone that melts into a wonderful consistency. If you don't have Gruyère, Swiss is nice, and cream cheese is fine in place of mascarpone. The basic idea is a full-flavored hard cheese and a sweeter, creamier cheese. The result is a creamy center and a really crunchy crust.

6 quarts water

2 tablespoons salt

1 pound rigatoni

1 pound bacon, diced

1 onion, diced

1 butternut squash, peeled and diced

2 cloves garlic, minced

3 tablespoons all-purpose flour

1 quart plus 3 cups half-and-half

1 cup Gruyère

Pinch of nutmeg

1 cup mascarpone

2 cups bread crumbs

1 bunch parsley, chopped

1. Preheat the oven to 375 °F.

2. Bring the water to a boil in a large pot. Add the salt. Cook the rigatoni in boiling water until tender but a little less cooked than the package instructions suggest. Drain, then set aside.

Less is more

There are few things worse than mac 'n' cheese where the pasta has cooked so long it just about disintegrates. Mario often says to cook your pasta for a minute less than it recommends on the box, and that's good advice for a pot-to-plate pasta dish, but in this casserole, the pasta is going to keep cooking, so I precook my pasta for 4 minutes less than recommended on the box before putting it in with the cheese and baking.

Make it healthier

Butternut squash or pumpkin baked into a mac 'n' cheese casserole adds sweetness, nutrients, and enough vegetables to make it a healthier one-course meal.

3. Cook the bacon until crisp. Sweat the onion, butternut squash, and garlic in a pan until translucent, then add flour to the pan to make roux. Slowly pour in the half-and-half while mixing, and bring mixture to simmer. Add in ½ cup of the Gruyère and nutmeg, and constantly stir until all the cheese is melted. Add the mascarpone, and mix until melted and combined. Add the cooked rigatoni and toss pasta until it's well mixed in the cheese mixture. Transfer to a 9 x 13 casserole dish.

4. In a medium mixing bowl, toss the bread crumbs, remaining Gruyère, and parsley. Sprinkle the bread crumb mixture over the casserole, and bake at 375 °F for 5–8 minutes, until the top is golden brown.

Travels well

There are few recipes more suited to a potluck dinner than mac 'n' cheese. Apart from the fact that everyone loves it, it is really easy to make at home and bring to a social gathering. Just cover it with plastic wrap and a rubber band to secure it, and it's ready to go. All that's needed to serve is reheating it in the oven when you reach your destination. And if the oven is too crowded, serve it as is. People will eat it. I promise.

Clinton gets the greatest Christmas present of his life: JoBeth Williams!

Clinton: When football season rolls around, there are somewhere between two and three million people cooking in parking lots outside of America's football stadiums: braising brats (that's bratwurst to you non-fans), slurping suds, killing kegs, roasting ribs, and making chili. If you can cook it for a long time with chili peppers, I guarantee you, somewhere in this great land of ours, some football fan is doing it. And since football brings out the competitive spirit, it is true that where there is chili, there are chili cook-offs, especially at Super Bowl time. So if you were asking yourself what kind of all-American cookbook would not have a chili cook-off, the answer is not this one.

Ladies and gentlemen, I give you a stalwart of the Seattle Seahawks, Mario Batali, and a son of the heartland and a bulwark of the Cleveland Browns, Michael Symon.

THE CHEW

Michael: It's a duel of the chilies. Looking to score some easy points, I figure Daphne is going to go for my chili because it's made with chicken so it's a little lighter.

Mario: I'm coming out all guns blazing with my Restrictor Plate Chili.

Michael: Sounds like something out of *The Terminator*. What's a restrictor plate?

Mario: It's something they put on really hot cars to slow them down on a small track. Likewise, my chili is so full of power, I need to contain it before it blows you away.

We both start with onions, because everything starts with onions, doesn't it?, and I throw in some bacon notably missing in Michael's recipe.

Michael: Hey, somebody stole my bacon!

Mario: You said you were going for a lighter chili, so I was only helping.

Michael: You know, one day I give up smoking and the next thing you know I'm making chicken chili and cutting down on the bacon. Am I on the road to becoming a vegan? But I am not cutting back on flavor, so I toss in coriander, cumin, cocoa, and then chipotle and smoked paprika.

The hot oil in the pan really makes those spices bloom. Great smell.

Mario: And the moment of truth as we add chilies to our chili. Michael . . . you first.

Michael: Chipotles and fresh serranos . . . good overall mouth heat, but not thermonuclear. And Mario, pride of the Northwest, what kind of chilies for you?

Mario: Well, I like hot, but I also like bright tanginess, so I'm going with pickled jalapeños.

Michael: Okay, Chef, now for the tomatoes and meat.

Mario: You mean chicken, don't you? Good red meat for me and chicken for you.

Michael: To amp up my guy points, I'm cooking in beer.

Mario: Back into your man cave, Cleveland Browns fan: I've got manliness to spare, enough so that I have the self-confidence to braise my chili in fresh pure water!

MICHAEL'S CHICKEN CHILI

SERVES 6 | **Skill Level: EASY** | **Cook Time: 2–2 ½ hrs.** | **Prep Time: 15 mins.** | **Cost: $**

5 tablespoons olive oil

2 pounds ground chicken

Salt, to taste

2 cups onion, diced small

3 cloves garlic, minced

2 serrano chilies, sliced into thin rings

1 tablespoon smoked paprika

2 tablespoons chili powder

2 tablespoons coriander, toasted and ground

1 tablespoon cumin, toasted and ground

1 teaspoon cayenne

1 12-ounce bottle beer (an IPA if possible)

1 14½-ounce can petite diced tomatoes

1 15-ounce can cannellini beans, drained and rinsed

1 15-ounce can red kidney beans, drained and rinsed

2 tablespoons brown sugar

2 teaspoons cocoa powder

2 cups water, plus 2 tablespoons

Chipotle hot sauce, to taste

7 ounces Greek yogurt

½ cup cilantro leaves, chopped

1. Heat a large Dutch oven over medium-high heat and add 3 tablespoons of the olive oil. When the oil is hot, add the ground chicken with a large pinch of salt and brown on all sides, breaking up the meat into smaller pieces as it cooks. Remove with a slotted spoon to a plate and set aside.

2. Drain the fat from the pot, then place back over the heat and add 2 tablespoons of olive oil. Reduce the heat to medium, and add the onion, garlic, and serranos with a small pinch of salt. Let the vegetables sweat for a few minutes, then add all of your spices. Toast them for about 30 seconds, being careful not to burn them.

3. Next, add the bottle of beer, making sure to scrape the bottom of the pot well. Add the meat back in along with the tomatoes and both beans.

4. Stir in the brown sugar, cocoa powder, and 2 cups of water, and reduce the heat to low. Season with some more salt and hot sauce to taste, and simmer, stirring occasionally, for 2 hours.

5. In the meantime, make the garnish by mixing together the yogurt and cilantro with a pinch of salt. Refrigerate until ready to use.

6. To serve, ladle some of the chili into bowls, garnishing with a big dollop of the yogurt.

MARIO'S RESTRICTOR PLATE CHILI

| SERVES 8 | Skill Level: EASY | Cook Time: 1 hr. | Prep Time: 20 mins. | Cost: $ |

6 slices bacon, cut into 1-inch pieces

2 onions, finely chopped

2 red bell peppers, stemmed, seeded, and finely chopped

6 cloves garlic, finely chopped

2 pounds ground sirloin

1 6-ounce can of tomato paste

¼ cup chili powder

2 tablespoons ground cumin

1 8-ounce can diced green chilies, drained

1 4-ounce can diced jalapeño chilies

4 cups water

1 28-ounce can crushed tomatoes

1 cup pitted green olives, coarsely chopped

1 teaspoon ground cinnamon

2 tablespoons dried oregano

1 12-ounce can pinto beans, drained

¾ cup fresh or frozen corn

8 8-inch flour tortillas

2 tablespoons olive oil

½ cup Cheddar cheese

¼ cup scallions, finely chopped

2 teaspoons cilantro

8 quail eggs

1. Place a large pot over medium-high heat and add the bacon pieces. When the bacon is cooked through, about 6 minutes, pour out some of the fat, add the onions and red bell peppers, and cook until the vegetables soften, about 6 minutes more. Add the garlic and cook for 1 minute more.

2. Add the ground sirloin and cook, breaking up the sirloin, until all the pink is gone, about 6 minutes more.

3. Add the tomato paste, chili powder, and ground cumin, and cook for 1 minute, stirring often.

4. Add the green chilies, jalapeños, water, tomatoes, olives, cinnamon, and oregano, and bring the liquid to a boil. Reduce the heat to medium-low, cover, and simmer the chili for 1 hour, stirring every 20 minutes or so to keep the bottom from scorching.

5. Add the pinto beans and corn, and simmer for 10 minutes more, stirring often. Remove from heat and serve, or let cool and keep cold in a refrigerator or ice-filled cooler for up to 3 days.

6. Brush the tortillas with olive oil. Fill with Cheddar, scallions, and cilantro, and grill until crispy on both sides, about 3–5 minutes.

7. Fry the quail eggs sunny-side up with a drizzle of olive oil in a pan.

8. Serve the chili with the quesadilla and quail egg.

Clinton: And now, in a less macho moment, it's the women's turn. First Carla:

Carla: I'm from Tennessee, which begins with *T* as in *Texas*, where they are the masters of cooking brisket. So I'll leave it to the boys as to who is more macho and simply point out that mine has a lot of hearty, manly—and, for that matter, me-big-strong-girl—beef.

My chili cooks for a long, long time in a low oven. For liquid, since I don't drink, I eat my alcohol and cook it off with beer. Ancho chilies give it beautiful heat, with a touch of sweetness. And finally, you know how in Mexico their most famous mole is made with chocolate? I figured, why not with chili? When you taste it, you'll see—no reason why not. Yum!!

CHILI CON CARLA

SERVES 8 | **Skill Level: EASY** | **Cook Time: 3½ –4 hrs.** | **Prep Time: 15 mins.** | **Cost: $**

6 large dried ancho chilies

2 tablespoons canola oil

1¼ pounds onions, chopped

1 5-pound flat-cut beef brisket, cut into 2½- to 3-inch cubes

Coarse kosher salt, to taste, plus 1½ teaspoons

Pepper, to taste

6 large cloves garlic, peeled

2 teaspoons cumin seeds

1 teaspoon ground coriander

1¾ cups fire-roasted diced tomatoes with green chilies

1 12-ounce bottle Mexican beer

1 7-ounce can roasted green chilies, diced

2 tablespoons chili powder

4 ounces dark chocolate, chopped

Red onion, sliced, to garnish

Avocado, diced, to garnish

Monterey Jack cheese, grated, to garnish

Tortillas, to garnish

Cilantro, to garnish

Sour cream, to garnish

1. Place the ancho chilies in a medium bowl. Pour enough boiling water to cover them and soak the chilies for about 4 hours, or until they are soft.

2. Preheat the oven to 350 °F.

3. In a large, ovenproof Dutch oven over medium-high heat, add 2 tablespoons canola oil and the onion and cook until translucent. Season the brisket liberally with salt and pepper. Add this to the pot and toss to coat with fat.

4. Drain the chilies, reserving the soaking liquid. Pour 1 cup of the soaking liquid, along with the chilies, into a blender with the garlic, cumin seeds, coriander, and salt. Blend until pureed, then add to the Dutch oven, along with the tomatoes, beer, green chilies, chili powder, and chocolate.

5. Stir and bring to a simmer, cover, and transfer to the oven. Cook for 2 hours, and then remove the lid and continue to cook for 45 minutes, until the brisket is almost tender. Skim the fat from the surface and add water, if necessary, to keep the brisket submerged. Cook an additional 45 minutes, until meat is tender.

6. To serve, spoon into bowls and top with desired garnishes.

Daphne: Mine is a total vegetarian chili, and it also happens to be a longtime favorite of the Oz family. I like to make it on Friday and let the flavors mingle and multiply until Sunday. It's always better when you let it sit and work its alchemy.

Carla has beer as her secret ingredient. So does Michael. When you think about it for a second, beer is probably the most common drink at tailgates, so why not go with the flow and toss it in your chili? Well, my extra-special super flavor-enhancing ingredient is tangy, smoky, hot chipotles in adobo. Don't let me forget the beans, as my cohost sister seems to have done. Whenever you order chili in a restaurant, it has beans, doesn't it? Full of protein, creaminess, and rib sticking enough to take the place of meat. There is so much power and flavor in this chili that I have seen 280-pound fullbacks eat it and smile with satisfaction.

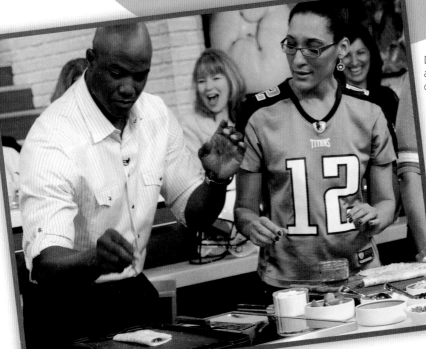

DeMarcus Ware adds a little spice like a true champion!

DAPHNE'S VEGGIE CHILI

SERVES 8 | Skill Level: EASY | Cook Time: 45 mins. | Prep Time: 10 mins. | Cost: $

2 tablespoons canola oil

1 large yellow onion, chopped

4 cloves garlic, smashed

2 medium zucchinis, sliced and diced

1 bag corn, frozen or fresh

2 tablespoons tomato paste

1 16-ounce can of roasted tomatoes, chopped, with juice

Salt

Pepper

2–3 bay leaves

2 tablespoons oregano

¼ cup chili powder

2–3 tablespoons cumin

1–2 chipotle peppers in adobo sauce, chopped

2 15-ounce cans kidney beans (drained and rinsed)

1 15-ounce can black beans (drained and rinsed)

1 12-ounce bottle beer

1 cup vegetable stock

Cheddar cheese, shredded, to serve

Avocado, chopped, to serve

Juice of 2 limes, to serve

Sour cream, to serve

1. In a large, heavy pot, heat the oil over medium-high heat.

2. Add the onion and garlic, and sauté until translucent.

3. Add the zucchini and corn, and sauté for 5 minutes, stirring occasionally.

4. Add the tomato paste and chopped tomatoes with their juice from the can. Then add the salt, pepper, herbs, and spices.

5. Add 1–2 chopped chipotle peppers and the beans. Stir well.

6. Add the beer and vegetable stock until liquid covers all ingredients in the pot.

7. Bring to a boil, and then reduce heat to medium-low. Simmer for a half hour, stirring occasionally. Remove from heat, and adjust seasonings to taste.

8. Serve with shredded Cheddar, chopped avocado, fresh lime juice, and sour cream.

Clinton: Before our cook-off chefs take off the pads and go at it bare knuckles, we'll leave this battle for the Champion of Chili and leave it to you to try to make your own call. If your Super Bowl party is big enough, make all four. You'll know who the winner is pretty easily. It's the pot that's empty at the end of the game.

WINTER

DEEP-DISH PIZZA CASSEROLE

| SERVES 10 | Skill Level: EASY | Cook Time: 40 mins. | Prep Time: 30 mins. | Cost: $ |

Inactive Prep Time: 12 hrs.

First an apology. "Chicago, I'm sorry." You see, when I think of pizza, the only thing that comes to mind is thin-crust pizza like they make in New York (and Naples, and Rome). The delicious food that they call deep-dish pizza is, to me, a casserole. Why? Because to my way of thinking, anything that you bake for more than 30 minutes crosses the line from pizza to casserole.

Glad I got that off my chest!

Mario suggested that I take full responsibility and call it—after my home-town—"Cleveland pizza."

Not going there. That would really get Chicago on my case. Basically, you take my pizza dough, line a casserole dish with it, and fill it with pureed San Marzano tomatoes, onions, ham, bacon, maybe a little sausage if you are feeling extra carnivorous, and lots of provolone and Parmigiano cheese. Or you could go vegetarian, leave out the meat and put in mushrooms, broccoli, or whatever strikes your fancy. Then call it whatever you want. I'm sure you'll be back for seconds.

FOR THE DOUGH:

1¼ teaspoons fresh yeast

3½ cups warm water

10 cups all-purpose flour

2¼ tablespoons kosher salt

Oil, for the bowl

FOR THE SAUCE:

1 15-ounce can San Marzano tomatoes, drained

2 cloves garlic

1 tablespoon dried oregano

1 tablespoon dried basil

Salt

Freshly ground black pepper

TO MAKE THE DOUGH:

1. In the bowl of your mixer, bloom the yeast in the water by mixing it in, breaking up any lumps, then letting it sit until it becomes slightly foamy and the water is cloudy, about 5 minutes.

2. Combine the flour and salt, then add to the bloomed yeast mixture. With the dough hook attachment for your mixer, mix on medium speed for 11 minutes. The dough should come together as one mass and begin climbing the hook.

3. After the dough has been mixed, turn it out into a lightly oiled mixing bowl, and let it proof until it is doubled in size. This should take a few hours, depending on how warm the air is. You should also cover the bowl with a damp cloth or plastic wrap during this process so it doesn't dry out.

FOR THE PIZZA:

2 tablespoons olive oil

4 pieces bacon, chopped

1 tablespoon butter

1 onion, chopped

¼ pound provolone, cut into thin slices

4 pieces good-quality ham, cut into strips

Freshly grated Parmigiano

Basil, to serve

4. After the dough has risen, portion it into 7–8 9-ounce balls. Place the portioned dough on a sheet tray with a piece of parchment paper that has been lightly oiled. Cover the sheet tray really well with plastic wrap and refrigerate overnight. The dough will be rested and ready to use the next day.

TO MAKE THE SAUCE:

5. Combine the drained tomatoes, garlic, and dried herbs in a blender or food processor. Pulse until the desired consistency. Pour into a bowl and season with salt and pepper.

TO MAKE THE PIZZA:

6. In a large sauté pan, heat the olive oil over medium-high heat. Add the bacon, and cook until crisp. Remove the bacon, leaving some of the fat behind. Add the butter and the onion, and cook until softened. Remove from heat and set aside.

7. On a floured work surface, roll out the dough into a ¼-inch-thick circle. In a 14-inch oiled cast-iron skillet, fit the dough inside and pinch around the top.

8. Add onions to the skillet. Next, add some of the bacon as a layer. Add a layer of provolone. Add a layer of ham, then pour the sauce over and sprinkle the Parmigiano over the sauce. Repeat the layers until the skillet is full. Bake for 25–30 minutes, until the crust is golden brown and cheese begins to bubble through the sauce. Let cool for about 10 minutes before serving. Garnish with basil.

MEATLOAF ALLA MARIO

SERVES 8 | **Skill Level: EASY** | **Cook Time: 1 hr. 30 mins.** | **Prep Time: 20 mins.** | **COST: $$**

Everyone has a favorite meatloaf recipe that their mom made. That kind of leaves me out because my mom wasn't a big meatloaf maker. But Grandma was a Meatloaf Mama from the get-go. Being of good Italian blood, she wasn't content with just throwing together some chopped meat, ketchup, and onions and calling it a recipe. She stuffed her meatloaf with wonderful vegetables and some mortadella and cheese. When I made this on the show, Carla pointed out—no doubt with her sense of the surreal—that this recipe will feed a group of 375 people. All I can say to Carla is, this is so delicious that a family of eight can work through it quite nicely.

2 pounds sweet Italian sausage, casings removed

2 pounds lean ground beef

4¼ cups fresh bread crumbs

2 cups freshly grated Pecorino Romano

3 eggs, lightly beaten

1 cup whole milk

Salt

Freshly ground black pepper

8 quarts plus 1 cup water

1 pound baby spinach, trimmed

4 carrots, peeled and cut lengthwise into strips

12 scallions, trimmed

¼ cup all-purpose flour, plus extra for dusting

10 pieces mortadella, sliced thin

6 slices Cacio di Roma

2 sprigs fresh rosemary

¾ cup extra virgin olive oil

1. Preheat the oven to 375 °F.

2. In a large bowl, combine the sausage, beef, 4 cups of the bread crumbs, the Pecorino Romano, eggs, milk, salt, and pepper. Mix gently but thoroughly with your hands. Cover and refrigerate.

3. Bring 8 quarts of water to a boil in a large pasta pot. Set up an ice bath nearby.

4. Add 2 tablespoons of salt to the boiling water. Dip the spinach leaves in the water just to wilt them, and immediately transfer them to the ice bath; then drain them in a colander. Add the carrots to the boiling water and cook for 10 minutes; then remove with a spider or slotted spoon and set aside. Drop the scallions in the boiling water and cook for 1 minute; then plunge them in the ice bath and let them cool for 1 minute. Drain and set on a towel-lined plate.

5. Combine the flour with the remaining ¼ cup bread crumbs, and heavily dust a wooden board or other work surface with the mixture. On the dusted board, pat the meat mixture into a 1½-inch-thick rectangle, about 6 by 16 inches. Place the spinach leaves between two plates and press them together to remove any remaining water, and then lay the spinach over the meat, leaving a 1-inch border on the short sides. Lay the carrot pieces and then the scallions over the spinach, arranging them lengthwise down the rectangle. Lay the mortadella and Cacio di Roma over the

scallions. Starting from a long side, roll the meat up like a jelly roll, making it as compact as possible; patch any holes like modeling clay. The roll should be about 16 inches long. Dust the outside with flour.

6. Place the loaf on a rimmed baking sheet. Press a sprig of rosemary into each side of the meatloaf, and pour 1 cup of water into the pan. Drizzle ½ cup of the olive oil down the length of the loaf. Bake the meatloaf for 1 hour 20 minutes, or until it reaches an internal temperature of 165 °F.

7. Carefully transfer the load to a cutting board and allow it to rest for 15 minutes.

8. Strain the pan juices into a saucepan and bring to a boil. Season with salt and pepper to taste, add the remaining ¼ cup oil, and whisk to form a loose sauce.

9. Slice the meatloaf into 1-inch-thick slices and arrange them on warmed plates. Drizzle with the sauce and serve.

CHOCAHOLIC WHOOPIE PIES

MAKES 36 | **Skill Level: EASY** | **Cook Time: 30 mins.** | **Prep Time: 20 mins.** | **Cost: $**

Spurred on by the nationwide cupcake craze, I wanted to do something a little different but just as easy—in fact easier. For those of you not from the Northeast, a whoopie pie is two chocolate cakes sandwiched around a layer of white filling. For the longest time, I have wondered why it's called whoopie pie. In Pennsylvania, they say it's an Amish invention, and that when Amish women would serve this, their menfolk would go, "Whoopie!" I think that's the PG version. I tend to side with Michael that whenever they ate this, they were ready to make whoopie. Michael got a little carried away, though, because when he learned that they take only a few minutes to make, he said, "Just like making whoopie!"

TMI, Michael.

FOR THE CAKES:

2 cups unbleached all-purpose flour

½ cup unsweetened cocoa (such as Droste)

½ teaspoon baking soda

½ teaspoon fine salt

Cinnamon, optional

1 stick unsalted butter at room temperature

1 cup granulated sugar

1 large egg

1 cup milk

FOR THE FILLING:

1 stick unsalted butter, softened

2 cups powdered sugar

½ teaspoon vanilla extract

1 cup mascarpone

½ cup white chocolate, melted

TO MAKE THE CAKES:

1. Arrange the oven racks in the upper and lower thirds of the oven, and preheat the oven to 425 °F. Line 2 large baking sheets with parchment paper.

2. Whisk together the flour, cocoa, baking soda, and salt in a medium bowl. You can add additional spices, like cinnamon, if you wish.

3. Cream the butter and sugar in the bowl of an electric mixer at high speed until fluffy, about 4 minutes. Add the egg, and beat at medium speed until incorporated. At low

speed, add the flour mixture in 2 batches, alternating with the milk, mixing until just blended.

4. Using a ½ tablespoon measure, drop 18 generous teaspoons of batter onto each sheet, leaving about 2 inches between cakes. Bake the 2 sheets at the same time, 5–7 minutes, until springy to touch. Let cool on the sheets for 5 minutes, and transfer to racks to cool completely. Change the parchment and repeat using the remaining batter (72 cakes in total).

TO MAKE THE FILLING:

5. Beat the butter and powdered sugar at low speed until blended, and then beat at high speed until fluffy, about 5 minutes. Add the vanilla and mascarpone, and mix at low speed until blended, about 1 minute. Slowly mix in the cooled melted white chocolate.

TO MAKE THE WHOOPIE PIES:

6. Match pairs of cake with the same shapes and spread the bottom side of 1 cake with filling (or use a piping bag), and sandwich together with the other cake. Store the finished whoopie pies in a covered plastic container and chill for up to 3 days.

GRILLED BACON, CHOCOLATE-HAZELNUT SANDWICH

MAKES 3 Sandwiches | Skill Level: EASY | Cook Time: 15 mins. | Prep Time: 5 mins. | Cost: $

I don't know what to call this: a dessert, a snack, or Falling Off the Dieting Wagon. It's one of my favorite midnight munchies. I got addicted to them when I was in high school. The combinations of salty and sweet, smooth and crispy . . . are the ones that most human beings find irresistible. I don't recommend it as part of any diet plan. On the other hand, a diet that doesn't take account of a very occasional indulgence is one that will soon be thrown in the dustbin of dining history. How about we make a deal? Have it every other weekend. Beware, though: once you buy a jar of the chocolate-hazelnut spread that I use for this, it will call to you in the middle of the night. Don't answer it.

½ **pound bacon**

½ **loaf Pullman bread or pain de mie**

½ **cup chocolate-hazelnut spread**

3 bananas

6 tablespoons butter

1. Preheat a skillet, and fry the bacon until crisp. When ready, transfer the bacon to a paper towel–lined plate to cool.

2. Slice the Pullman loaf into 6 ½-inch slices, and spread a tablespoon, give or take, of the chocolate-hazelnut spread onto each of the slices. Slice the bananas lengthwise and then in half, and add 4 slices to each sandwich. Arrange 3 slices of bacon onto the banana slices, and make a sandwich. Generously butter both sides of each sandwich.

3. In a preheated nonstick skillet over medium heat, grill the sandwiches on either side, until golden brown, and serve.

Valentine's at Our House

Clinton

Today is the day for lovers and, if you make the right meal, the night for loving. We asked our Chewster Board of Romantic Knowledge about food and love on the same day.

Mario

The way to impress someone is to make something that is delicious and kind of erotic and sexy yet very simple, so you look good when you make it, it's delicious, and the payoff is immense.

Carla

Tell you the truth, I pretty much always worked on Valentine's Day, so whatever I do, I do just for my husband. I make something that is nice and light so that when you wanna get busy later, you still have the energy to do it! This year, I think I'm gonna do something really special, like put on an old-fashioned Pan Am stewardess outfit. I'll put that on . . . and . . .

Clinton

TMI, Carla.

Mario

Word, Carla! With Valentine's dinner, make sure you leave some of the food on the plate. The "Clean Plate Club" never needs to exist on Valentine's Day. Because you should be focused on other things!

Michael

In Cleveland, because Hallmark and American Greeting cards are there, we have a lot of those Hallmark holidays. We go out with our kids. Because we all love each other so much, we think it's a family date, not a man/woman or a spouse/spouse date. We traditionally get cheese fondue and then chocolate fondue.

Daphne

I make a meal that's all red things. I do a red main course, a red salad with beets. I do a red dessert with strawberries and a red velvet cake, so it's all red! Maybe I'll cheat a little with some pink Champagne.

Mario presents a Valentine's Day rose to Jewel.

Clinton

You're all so thoughtful! We don't do anything at my house because each day is Valentine's Day!

HOT MUTTERED BUM

SERVES 4 | **Skill Level: EASY** | **Inactive Cook Time: 5 hrs.** | **Prep Time: 5 mins.** | **Cost: $**

There may not be a cure for the common cold, but this drink is a killer of the winter blues. What makes it different from the classic hot buttered rum is that I put all the ingredients, except for the rum, in a slow cooker for 4–6 hours. You have to add the rum at the end, otherwise the alcohol cooks away and your cocktail becomes a mocktail. This was so good that Mario growled like a lion (although he was about as convincing as Bert Lahr in The Wizard of Oz).

2 cups dark brown sugar

½ cup butter

1 teaspoon salt

1 teaspoon vanilla extract

2 quarts hot water

3 cinnamon sticks

6 whole cloves

2 cups spiced rum

1 cup sweetened whipped cream

¼ teaspoon ground nutmeg

1. Combine the dark brown sugar, butter, salt, vanilla extract, and hot water in a slow cooker. Add the cinnamon sticks and cloves. Cover and cook on low for 5 hours. Stir in the rum.

2. Ladle from the slow cooker into mugs, and top with whipped cream and a dusting of nutmeg.

ROLES ROYCE

SERVES 10 | **Skill Level: EASY** | **Prep Time: 5 mins.** | **Cost: $**

I made this in honor of Cheryl Hines for her character on Suburgatory, *Dallas Royce. (Get it? Her role is Royce.) It is a super holiday punch: deep red cranberry juice swirling in a sea of black currant-rich cassis and luxurious Champagne. The great thing about this punch—make that all punches—is if you are the host, you are not stuck playing bartender to a roomful of demanding guests who want their drinks just so.*

8 cups cranberry juice

2 bottles dry Champagne or sparkling wine

3 cups crème de cassis (black currant–flavored liqueur)

4 cups seltzer

Lemon peel for garnish

1. Combine ingredients in a punch bowl. Garnish each glass with a lemon peel and serve.

WINTER

113

POTATO LEEK SOUP

| SERVES 4 | Skill Level: EASY | Cook Time: 30 mins. | Prep Time: 10 mins. | COST: $ |

I made this for our St. Patrick's Day show and, as I told the audience, "It's so good you are going to want to kiss the Blarney Stone!" Usually by the time St. Paddy's Day rolls around, I've had it up to my eyeballs with Old Man Winter. There are few things that fight off the chill like a spud-based soup. Top it with some good Irish Cheddar and crumbled bacon.

FOR THE SOUP:

Extra virgin olive oil

1 onion, diced

2 leeks, washed and sliced

2 stalks celery, chopped

1 clove garlic, minced

4 cups chicken stock

2 cups milk

1 bay leaf

4 Yukon gold potatoes, peeled and cubed

Salt

Freshly ground pepper

2 tablespoons fresh parsley, chopped

½ cup half-and-half

1 cup bacon, fried crisp and chopped into small pieces, for garnish

FOR THE IRISH CHEDDAR CROUTONS:

4 thin slices Irish Cheddar cheese

4 slices country bread, toasted golden brown

1. In a large stockpot, heat the oil over medium-high heat. Add the onion, leeks, celery, and garlic, and cook until all have softened and become fragrant, about 5 minutes. Add the stock, milk, bay leaf, and potatoes, and season with salt and pepper. Bring to a simmer. Cook until the potatoes are tender, about 25 minutes. Stir in the parsley and half-and-half. Allow to cool slightly. In batches, puree in a blender.

2. Serve with the Irish Cheddar croutons and sprinkle with bacon.

TO MAKE THE IRISH CHEDDAR CROUTONS:

3. Preheat the broiler and place the cheese slices on the toasted bread. Broil until the cheese is melted and browned in spots, about 2–3 minutes.

Grit ain't great

Because of the kind of soil they are grown in, leeks can be quite sandy and gritty. That's no fun. To get rid of grittiness, I recommend slicing leeks and putting them in a bowl filled with cold water. Slosh the sliced leeks around and the grit will fall to the bottom.

Gordon Elliott brings a dramatic flair to the stage.

Isn't bacon a vegetable?

Instead of using chicken stock, use vegetable stock to make this a vegetarian recipe. I guess you'll have to skip the bacon, although I kind of think bacon always gets a free pass. I think we should make it an honorary vegetable.

IRISH SODA BREAD

SERVES 8 | **Skill Level: EASY** | **Cook Time: 1 hr. 10 mins.** | **Prep Time: 15 mins.** | **Cost: $**

St. Paddy's Day without soda bread is like the Fourth of July without fireworks. So dipping down into the Irish part of my soul—and on St. Patrick's Day, we're all a little Irish—I offer you this quick bread. I say quick because there is no yeast, no waiting hours for the bread to rise, and no kneading. Buttermilk gives it extra depth and the mouth-fillingness of the best southern biscuits. Serve warm and slather with Irish butter or melted Irish Cheddar. Then make a wish on a shamrock!

½ cup unsalted butter, cut into cubes, plus 1 tablespoon and to serve

5 cups all-purpose flour

1 cup sugar

1 tablespoon baking powder

½ teaspoon baking soda

1½ teaspoons salt

2½ cups golden raisins

Zest of 1 orange

2½ cups buttermilk

1 large egg

1. Preheat the oven to 350 °F.

2. Butter a 10-inch cast-iron skillet with 1 tablespoon of butter and set aside.

3. In a large bowl combine the all-purpose flour, sugar, baking powder, baking soda, and salt. Add remaining butter and the orange zest. Using your fingertips, combine until the mixture resembles wet sand. Stir in the raisins.

4. In a separate bowl, whisk together the buttermilk and egg, and fold into the flour mixture using a wooden spoon.

5. Transfer the dough to the prepared skillet. Smooth the top, mounding slightly in center. Dip a knife in flour and mark an X on the top of the batter.

6. Bake until bread is cooked through and a toothpick inserted into the center comes out clean, about 1 hour 10 minutes. Cool bread in skillet for 10 minutes.

7. Serve with butter or melted Irish Cheddar.

SUPER BOWL PUNCH

SERVES 8 | **Skill Level: EASY** | **Prep Time: 10 mins.** | **Cost: $**

For our Super Bowl show, our tasting panel included some NFL greats: Dwight Freeney, DeMarcus Ware, and a member of my NFL Hall of Fame, the great Joe Theismann. We did some world championship cocktail tasting and ended up with my trademark Super Bowl Punch. It's a super easy recipe to remember because basically it's one cup of everything. I don't know if it's because we were so buzzed by the time we drank it, but when we all voted on our fave cocktail at the end of the show, the Super Bowl Punch came out on top.

1 cup vodka
1 cup tequila
1 cup rum
1 cup gin
1 cup triple sec
1 cup fresh lime juice
2 cups cranberry juice
4¼ cups ginger ale
2 cups blueberries
2 cups sliced strawberries

1. Combine alcohol and juice in a large punch bowl. Top with the ginger ale, and stir in the blueberries and strawberries.

2. When ladling out to guests, top glasses with a touch more fizz on top.

THE WARM AND TOASTY

SERVES 1 | Skill Level: EASY | Prep Time: 15 mins. | Cook Time: 5 mins. | Cost: $

I suppose if you drink enough of my version of Irish coffee, you could call your-self "warm and toasty" or "hot and plastered." Since people really like hazelnut coffee these days, I put in some hazelnut liqueur (think of it as liquid Nutella). Of course you need Irish cream and—to give you a little jolt—some nice, strong coffee. After three of these, I guarantee you'll be having a nice chat with a lepre-chaun who strolled into your cocktail party.

¾ **cup brewed coffee**

1 **ounce hazelnut liqueur**

1 **ounce Irish cream**

1½ **ounces whipped cream**

Chocolate shavings, to garnish

1. Pour coffee into a mug. Add the hazelnut liqueur. Finally add the Irish cream and stir.

2. Top with the whipped cream and chocolate shavings.

WINTER

SPICY GRAPEFRUIT MARGARITA, AKA "THE CLINTON CALIENTE"

| SERVES 1 | Skill Level: EASY | Cook Time: 15 mins. | Prep Time: 25 mins. | Cost: $ |

Inactive Prep Time: 12 hrs.

There is an old saying: "If it ain't broke, don't fix it." True enough, but if the classic margarita is great, then so is the idea of seeing what else you can do with it that is equally delicious. My solution is to add some habañero peppers in the salt that rims the glass and in the ice cubes. I guarantee they'll be the hottest cubes you ever taste. Also, some grapefruit juice in the cubes, when mixed with your tequila, gives it some fruitiness and a dash of bitter taste that balances the sweetness of the simple syrup and orange liqueur in the classic margarita. I'm sure the Mayor of Margaritaville, Jimmy Buffett, would approve.

FOR THE SPICY SALT:

Kosher salt

1 habañero, sliced

FOR THE SIMPLE SYRUP:

1 cup sugar

1 cup water

1 habañero, sliced

FOR THE ICE CUBES:

Habañero slices (from the simple syrup recipe)

1 grapefruit, sliced into small wedges or quarters

Water

FOR THE MARGARITA:

2 ounces tequila

2 ounces fresh pink grapefruit juice

1 ounce orange liqueur

½–1 ounce spicy simple syrup

2 ice cubes

FOR THE SPICY SALT:

1. Combine salt and habañero in a food processor. Grind together and set aside.

FOR THE SIMPLE SYRUP:

2. In a small sauce pot add sugar and water. Cook over medium heat until sugar has dissolved into the water. Add the habañero and steep for a few minutes. Strain out the habañero slices and reserve on a separate plate. Set the simple syrup aside to cool.

FOR THE ICE CUBES:

3. In each cavity of an ice cube tray add a slice of grapefruit and a slice of habañero pepper (reserved from making the simple syrup). Fill tray with water and freeze overnight.

FOR MARGARITA:

4. Dip glass in salt to cover the rim. Combine the tequila, grapefruit juice, orange liqueur, and simple syrup in a cocktail shaker. Shake to combine and strain into a salted rocks glass. Add ice cubes and serve.

SPRING

SPICY SHRIMP COCKTAIL, 128 | RICOTTA, MINT, AND SPRING PEA BRUSCHETTA, 129 | CARROTS WITH FETA AND MINT, 130 | SPRING VEGETABLE PASTA WITH CHIVE BREAD CRUMBS, 133 | BACON, EGG, AND CHEESE CASSEROLE, 134 | ASPARAGUS AND GOAT CHEESE FRITTATA, 136 | ROMAN-STYLE ARTICHOKES, 137 | GRILLED SALMON WITH SHAVED CARROTS AND PEANUT SALAD, 138 | BEER-BATTERED FISH AND CHIPS, 140 | MOM'S CHICKEN WITH SAFFRON, OLIVES, AND ONIONS, 142 | BIG TURKEY MEATBALL SUBS, 143 | PAELLA, 146 | CURRIED CHICKEN AND DUMPLINGS, 148 | GREEK EASTER LEG OF LAMB, 149 | POT ROAST WITH SHAVED CARROT SALAD, 152 | BAHN MI, 153 | RED VELVET CAKE, 154 | SEBADAS, 156 | SWEET PHYLLO PACKETS, 157 | COCONUT PECAN POUND CAKE, 159 | BANANA PUDDIN, 160 | MINT JULEP, 162 | STRAWBERRY WHITE WINE COOLER PUNCH, 163 | RHUBARB PUNCH, 164

Q&A
WITH
Daphne

Q: **In a sense . . . you're the voice of the viewer who looks at food in terms of their family experience, usually with Mom.**

Daphne: One of the things I loved about how my mom cooked is we would look through a cookbook together and then we'd go food shopping and get a bunch of ingredients and then we'd never look at the recipe again! She'd add this spice and that, she'd go by her tongue, she'd teach me how to find the flavor pairings that made sense, even if they aren't traditional. Now when I am on the show presenting recipes that I grew up on, I am literally sharing a piece of my home and family.

Q: **How does it feel to be cooking alongside famous TV and restaurant chefs?**

Daphne: I am especially grateful for the way they won't ever let you mess up. Before we do a segment together, Mario always tells me, "I've got your back." Literally, every single time. And he does! He makes sure the recipe

SPRING

125

is the way it should be. If I miss something or if the way that I make it isn't right, he adds those pointers in, and it's great to learn from someone who's had that level of mastery in his career.

Q: **What do you take away from your experience on the show?**

Daphne: What I love being reminded of daily is that it's okay to mess up. Even the professionals who have been doing it for thirty years mess up, as when Michael messed up his omelet and Mario's burnt things and Carla's burnt things and Clinton's burnt things. It happens, and there are ways you can recover. I learn something, a kernel of truth about cooking, every single day; things like "don't overwork your biscuits" or "don't load the pan with too many mushrooms or they'll steam and they won't come out with the best texture." It's those little things that you want people to take away, because it'll make home cooking different and better.

Q: **How about yourself as the health expert on the show?**

Daphne: Having struggled with my weight all throughout childhood and in a fairly health-conscious family, I came with a commitment to make health a priority and not simply losing weight and fad dieting.

I'm always looking for those ways to strip down calories and fat, always asking, "How are we going to enjoy our food and put a priority on health?" But I would never recommend artificial sweeteners or lower-grade oils just to save calories, because at the end of the day, we are trying to send a message about enjoying food.

If there is one thing I would like viewers to remember is the less processed it is, the better it is for you no matter what. Even if it's very high fat, high calorie, very calorie dense. I would always have whole milk instead of skim, and I'll have less of it. I would always have real sugar or real honey or maple syrup or whatever, rather than some no-cal sweetener that may or may not be a carcinogen. What we try to point you toward is things you're going to find in your supermarket, if not already in your refrigerator, and then some creative ways to put them together that will bring more pleasure to your table in a healthy way.

SPICY SHRIMP COCKTAIL

SERVES 4 | **Skill Level: EASY** | **Cook Time: 15 mins.** | **Prep Time: 15 mins.** | **Cost: $$**

I've been making this shrimp cocktail this way since the 1980s. It's probably as much a part of my identity as my orange Crocs. My humble addition to the noble traditions of shrimp cocktail-dom is a lot of peppercorns in the poaching liquids and the bite of serrano chili and scallions in the sauce. Just writing these words makes me want a glass of cold beer, so I guess it goes well with beer.

FOR THE SHRIMP:

2 tablespoons whole black peppercorns

5 sprigs fresh thyme

½ bunch parsley (leaves and stems)

1 lemon, halved

2 bay leaves

3 tablespoons kosher salt

3 quarts water

12 colossal shrimp, heads removed

FOR THE COCKTAIL SAUCE:

½ cup ketchup

¼ cup fresh horseradish (or 2 tablespoons prepared)

Juice and zest of 1 lemon

1 tablespoon Worcestershire sauce

1 serrano chili, seeded and finely minced

2 scallions, minced

1 teaspoon kosher salt

TO MAKE THE SHRIMP:

1. Combine the peppercorns, thyme, parsley, lemon, bay leaves, and salt in a large pot filled with 3 quarts of water. Bring to a boil.

2. Drop the shrimp into the water and lower the heat to a simmer, stirring occasionally. Simmer until the shrimp turn pink and curl slightly, about 4–6 minutes. Remove the shrimp from the cooking liquid and cool to room temperature. Once cool enough to handle, remove the shells from the shrimp, leaving the tails intact. Refrigerate until ready to serve.

TO MAKE THE COCKTAIL SAUCE:

3. Whisk together the ketchup, horseradish, lemon juice and zest, and Worcestershire sauce. Fold in the serrano and the scallions. Season with salt, and serve alongside the shrimp.

RICOTTA, MINT, AND SPRING PEA BRUSCHETTA

SERVES 6 | Skill Level: EASY | Cook Time: 5 mins. | Prep Time: 10 mins. | Cost: $

Bruschetta: that's Italian for something delicious on toast. Actually, I don't know what it literally means in Italian, but every bruschetta I have ever seen is something great on toast. This recipe is my way to welcome spring. It also revealed another side to the ever-fascinating Carla. That woman loves her peas! When we made this on the show, she snatched the whole bowl of peas and stuffed about a hundred in her mouth before I could rescue enough to make this recipe.

4 cups shelled English peas

1–2 teaspoons kosher salt

2 cups fresh sheep's milk ricotta cheese

Zest of 1 lemon

3 tablespoons grated Parmesan

¼ cup fresh mint leaves

Freshly ground black pepper

½ teaspoon red pepper flakes

¼ cup extra virgin olive oil

1 baguette, cut into ½-inch slices at a bias

1. Bring 1 gallon of water to a boil and add a large pinch of salt. Add the peas and blanch for about 30 seconds. Remove the peas to an ice bath.

2. To a food processor, add the ricotta, lemon zest, Parmesan, and mint. Drain the peas and add them to the food processor. Pulse just until the mixture becomes smooth, scraping down the sides from time to time.

3. Spoon the mixture into a serving bowl, crack some black pepper over the top, sprinkle with the red pepper flakes, and drizzle with extra virgin olive oil.

4. Heat a grill pan to medium-high. Brush the pieces of bread with olive oil and season with salt and pepper. Grill on each side until crisp and grill marks appear, about 1–2 minutes per side.

5. Serve each crostini topped with the pea mixture.

Stay seasonal

Eating seasonally and locally is always a good idea with fruits and vegetables. More flavor, better texture. With peas it's really important, because fresh green peas are super sweet. Leave them a few days and they get starchy.

Blanching is better

Blanching is a time-honored method for boosting green in fresh vegetables. With peas it also changes starchiness to sweetness. Spring peas are so tender and green, you really want to accent their sweetness.

CARROTS WITH FETA AND MINT

SERVES 4 | **Skill Level: EASY** | **Cook Time: 20–30 mins.** | **Prep Time: 5 mins.** | **Cost: $**

This dish is inspired by my mom, who was no doubt inspired by her mom: in other words, it's Greek. Feta cheese and mint are a classic combination with charred pan-roasted carrots. Cumin is a traditional partner for carrots as well, and so is the orange juice that I add to my vinaigrette. I leave the skins on the carrots because they really pick up the char well when the sugar in the carrots superheats in the pan. Dressing the carrots when they are hot allows them to soak up some of the vinaigrette. The flavors are so big that this recipe works as an appetizer all on its own, or as a side to roasted lamb or fish grilled over a wood fire.

1½ pounds carrots, cut into 2-inch chunks at a bias

1 teaspoon honey

2 tablespoons sherry vinegar

1 tablespoon whole cumin seeds, toasted

3 tablespoons extra virgin olive oil

Kosher salt

Freshly ground black pepper

FOR THE DRESSING:

¼ cup extra virgin olive oil

Zest and juice of 1 orange

1 tablespoon honey

1 tablespoon sherry vinegar

¼ cup mint (leaves only)

1 shallot, thinly sliced

¼ cup slivered almonds

Pinch of kosher salt

1 cup feta, crumbled, to serve

1 teaspoon orange zest, to serve

Olive oil, to serve

1. Preheat the oven to 450 °F.

2. In a mixing bowl, add the carrots and toss with the honey, vinegar, cumin seeds, and 1 tablespoon of olive oil.

3. In an oven-safe skillet over medium-high heat, heat the remaining olive oil, then add the carrots. Season generously with salt and pepper, and then toss to coat. Transfer to the oven and roast for 20 minutes, or until the carrots have caramelized and browned in spots.

4. Meanwhile, make the dressing by whisking together the extra virgin olive oil, orange juice and zest, honey, vinegar, mint leaves, shallot, and almonds. Add a pinch of salt and set aside.

5. Once the carrots have finished and cooled slightly, toss them in a large bowl with the dressing. To serve, garnish carrots with feta, orange zest, and a drizzle of olive oil.

Wonderful water

I always put a little pasta water in my pan sauce when it gets to the finishing stages. The starch in the water thickens the pan sauce so that it clings to the pasta.

Favas: to peel or not to peel?

If I'm making them on TV or in a restaurant, I peel them. At home, it's purely a question of how ambitious I feel. Most of the time I shuck the favas but don't peel each individual bean. I guess it also depends what's on TV. Peeling beans while you're watching something isn't a big deal.

SPRING VEGETABLE PASTA WITH CHIVE BREAD CRUMBS

SERVES 4 | **Skill Level: EASY** | **Cook Time: 15 mins.** | **Prep Time: 10 mins.** | **Cost: $**

Spring can't come fast enough in the Midwest. That's probably true everywhere, but all I know is that when I start to see asparagus and favas and peas in the markets in Cleveland, my spirits improve. The flowers are starting to pop. The pretty girls aren't so covered up. I can't get enough of spring or spring vegetables, so why not use them all at once? This pasta with a quick pan sauce is my version of spring training. It gets me back into cooking fresh green things. When I made this on the show, we nearly had to physically restrain Carla from rushing the serving bowl and devouring the whole thing. For sure, it's a lot for one person to eat, but Carla is a dedicated diner.

FOR THE CHIVE BREAD CRUMBS:

1 tablespoon olive oil

1 cup bread crumbs

¼ cup minced chives

Zest of 1 lemon

2 tablespoons Parmesan cheese

Salt

FOR THE SPRING PASTA:

1 pound fresh linguini pasta

Salt

2 tablespoons olive oil, plus extra to drizzle

2 cloves garlic, minced

1 bunch asparagus, chopped

½ pound fava beans, shelled and blanched

½ pound English peas, blanched

Parmesan cheese, to taste

2 tablespoons butter

1. Place a saucepan over medium-high heat and add the olive oil. Toss in the bread crumbs and cook until golden brown, about 3 minutes, stirring constantly. Remove from the heat and, in a mixing bowl, stir in the chives, zest, and the cheese. Season with salt and set aside.

2. Bring a large pot of water to a boil and add a generous pinch of salt. Cook the pasta 1 or 2 minutes less than the package instructions suggest.

3. Heat a large sauté pan over medium-high heat and add the olive oil. Once hot, add the garlic and the asparagus and season with salt.

4. Add in the fava beans and peas. Add a ladle of pasta water to the pot along with the cooked pasta. Toss to coat, and season again with salt, add some freshly grated Parmesan, the butter, and a drizzle of olive oil. Top with the chive bread crumbs and serve.

Extra virgin sometimes equals extra flavor

I use extra virgin olive oil to sauté my vegetables. Usually I don't recommend this because extra virgin (or EVOO, as cookbooks usually abbreviate it) smokes easily. But by cooking over medium heat for a short while, which is all that tender spring vegetables need, you get that extra floral whiff that only EVOO can give.

BACON, EGG, AND CHEESE CASSEROLE

SERVES 8 | Skill Level: EASY | Cook Time: 50 mins. | Prep Time: 30 mins. | Cost: $

Bacon, egg, and cheese on a biscuit always calls my name when I'm at a drive-through. That thought gave birth to this casserole. It's really perfect to serve for Sunday breakfast when you have people staying over. I start with your basic biscuit with some chives and cheese baked in. They need to be small, about the diameter of a golf ball. Then you layer in lots of bacon and lots of cheese and top with more biscuits. Finally, add the eggs and let it sit awhile so all the ingredients can get to know one another.

CHEDDAR CHIVE BISCUITS:

2 cups all-purpose flour

1 tablespoon baking powder

1 teaspoon sugar

¼ teaspoon baking soda

½ teaspoon salt

6 tablespoons unsalted butter, chilled and cut into cubes

¾ cup buttermilk

½ cup chives, chopped

¾ cup Cheddar cheese, shredded

CASSEROLE:

1 batch Cheddar Chive Biscuits

1 pound bacon, cooked and chopped

½ cup Cheddar cheese, grated

6 large eggs

1½ cups milk

½ cup chives, chopped

Salt and pepper to taste

FOR THE CHEDDAR CHIVE BISCUITS

1. Preheat the oven to 425 °F. In a large bowl, combine flour, baking powder, sugar, baking soda, and salt. Whisk until well combined. Into the dry mixture, cut in chilled cubes of butter. Texture should resemble small pebbles. Pour buttermilk over mixture, fold in chives, and gently stir to combine. Pour mixture out onto a lightly floured surface. Knead mixture just until dough comes together. Roll out dough to ⅓-inch thickness. Using a 1½-inch ring mold, cut out biscuits. Repeat process; be careful not to over-knead dough. Top each biscuit with Cheddar cheese. Place on a prepared baking sheet, bake for 8 minutes or until golden brown.

Cover up

I bake this in a medium oven and always cover my casserole with tin foil so that the eggs don't get too brown on top. You want a nice custardy interior.

When you add vegetables to a casserole—and you certainly could to this one—remember that vegetables are mostly water and you don't want a soupy casserole. You need to chop vegetables so that they are the same size (meaning they will be uniformly cooked) and cook them *before* you put them in the casserole. That way they have given up their water and your casserole holds together.

FOR THE CASSEROLE

2. Lower the oven to 350 °F. Butter a 9 x 13-inch casserole dish. Halve all biscuits. Place a single layer of Cheddar Chive Biscuit halves (the bottoms) into the casserole dish. Cover the biscuits with cooked and chopped bacon. Sprinkle Cheddar cheese over the bacon layer. Place biscuit tops over the cheese. In a large bowl, whisk together eggs, milk, chives, salt, and pepper. Pour egg mixture over biscuits. Cover and refrigerate for 30 minutes, allowing the egg custard to absorb into the biscuits. Bake, covered in foil, for 35–45 minutes until set.

ASPARAGUS AND GOAT CHEESE FRITTATA

SERVES 8 TO 10 | Skill Level: EASY | Cook Time: 20 mins. | Prep Time: 10 mins. | Cost: $

I'm pretty religious about making a frittata every Sunday that I'm home. If you ask me what I put in a frittata, my answer is (like it is for so much in cooking): "Whatever looks good in the market." I always celebrate the arrival of spring with asparagus in my frittata. Around that time, on the banks of rivers and streams around Cleveland, you can pick wild ramps. And soon after the ramps sprout, if we are very lucky and if the weather gods have treated us right, there might even be some wild morels. I'm going to figure that you aren't planning on a foraged frittata, so stick with the asparagus.

1 dozen eggs

½ cup heavy cream

2 tablespoons unsalted butter

1 shallot, minced

1½ pounds asparagus, trimmed and cut into 2-inch pieces

2 teaspoons kosher salt

½ teaspoon coarse ground black pepper

8 ounces soft goat cheese at room temperature

2 tablespoons tarragon, chopped

1. Preheat the oven to 375 °F.

2. In a large bowl, whisk together the eggs and the heavy cream, and set aside.

3. Melt the butter in a 10-inch cast-iron skillet or a non-stick oven-safe pan over medium heat. Add the shallot to the pan and sauté for 2 minutes, then add the asparagus. Season with the salt and pepper, and cook for 3 more minutes, until the asparagus has turned bright green but has not browned.

4. Add the egg and cream mixture, and pull a rubber spatula along the bottom of the pan until the eggs begin to scramble, about 3 minutes. Once the eggs begin to set, remove the pan from the heat and sprinkle in chunks of the goat cheese and the chopped tarragon. Place the pan in the oven and cook for about 15 minutes, or until the center is set but still jiggles slightly when you shake the pan.

5. Cut the frittata into 8–10 pieces and serve.

ROMAN-STYLE ARTICHOKES

SERVES 6 | Skill Level: EASY | Cook Time: 45 mins. | Prep Time: 20 mins. | Cost: $

There's nothing more Roman than artichokes braised in wine, olive oil, and seasonings, especially when you buy them all peeled and trimmed the way they do it for you in Rome. No such luck here in the States. You have to be your own artichoke trimmer. But it's really not that hard. Then pop them in the pot, toss in seasonings, some onion, garlic, fresh herbs—whatever you like—bring it to a boil, and then simmer for 15 minutes. The result: succulent, slithery, smoothness that boldly declares, "Arrivederci, Winter, Spring has finally sprung."

6 young artichokes

Juice of 2 lemons

¾ cup dry white wine

¾ cup boiling water

¾ cup extra virgin olive oil

Pinch of kosher salt

¼ bunch fresh parsley leaves

¼ bunch fresh mint leaves

2 cloves garlic, finely chopped

½ red onion, sliced

1 teaspoon chili flakes

1. Trim the artichokes of their tough outer leaves and cut in half. Remove the fuzzy choke with a spoon and place immediately in a bowl filled with water and the juice of one of the lemons.

2. Arrange all the chokes in a deep pan that keeps them close together.

3. Add the wine, boiling water, oil, and a pinch of salt.

4. Sprinkle the parsley, mint, garlic, red onion, and chili flakes over the top.

5. Squeeze the other lemon over the top, cover, and simmer on the stovetop for 25–30 minutes. Serve hot or at room temperature.

Tip

The braising liquid picks up wonderful flavor from the artichokes. Don't toss it. Use it to braise fennel, carrots, onions, string beans—whatever vegetable strikes your fancy.

Staying green: the acid test

To keep your nicely trimmed artichokes from turning gray, put them in an ice water bath with lemon juice or vinegar.

GRILLED SALMON WITH SHAVED CARROTS AND PEANUT SALAD

SERVES 4 | **Skill Level: EASY** | **Cook Time: 5 mins.** | **Prep Time: 5 mins.** | **Cost: $**

I made this when Hugh Jackman visited The Chew. *He said this combination of fresh salmon, fresh vegetables, and nuts is something his coach recommends when he's training for the role of Wolverine. That's some serious training! Cooking salmon to rare or medium rare is perfect for people who don't love "fishy fish." It's a lot milder and more buttery. Serving up raw vegetables with fish, poultry, or meat, is one of my favorite things and it definitely keeps the prep time down.*

4 6-ounce fillets of salmon, skin on

2 teaspoons salt

½ teaspoon fresh ground black pepper

¼ cup, plus 2 tablespoons extra virgin olive oil

3 medium organic carrots, peeled

1 tablespoon cumin seeds, toasted

1 bunch scallions, thinly sliced

1 cup mint leaves

½ cup toasted peanuts

2 tablespoons red wine vinegar

1. Season the salmon with 1 teaspoon salt and ½ teaspoon pepper, then brush with 2 tablespoons olive oil and grill for 2 minutes per side.

2. While the salmon is grilling, shave the carrots with a peeler or mandolin and add to a large bowl. Add the cumin seeds, scallions, mint, and peanuts.

3. In a separate bowl, whisk together the remaining olive oil and red wine vinegar, and add to the shaved vegetables.

4. Season liberally with salt and pepper. Place the salmon on a platter and top with the shaved carrot salad.

Don't flip out over flipping

The key to making fish on the grill is not to flip it too quickly or it will stick. For a piece of fish like this salmon, about 1½ inches thick, if you leave it for 2 minutes, it will crisp up nicely and not stick or tear when you flip it.

Roast and toast your spices

This recipe calls for cumin. With all aromatic spices, you'll find if you pan roast just before you use them, you release all the delicious, flavorful, fragrant oils that create intense flavor.

Hugh Jackman brings his charm to the crew.

BEER-BATTERED FISH AND CHIPS

SERVES 4 | Skill Level: EASY | Cook Time: 8–10 mins. | Prep Time: 20 mins. | Cost: $

Fish and chips are about the most favorite foods in England, Scotland, and Ireland. America sure has millions of people with that heritage. Still, many people have a fear of frying. There's no reason. If you make your batter right, get the oil to the correct temperature (about 360 °F), and don't over fry, you will have a crunchy crust and succulent fish. Just follow these instructions and I give you my triple money-back guarantee that it will turn out great. Wait . . . there's more! As a bonus, I'll toss in my secret to waking up the flavor in your batter: grate in some orange zest.

4 cups Wondra flour, plus 1 cup for dredging

1 tablespoon baking powder

½ teaspoon baking soda

2 tablespoons cornstarch

3 eggs

1½ cups milk

¾ cup wheat beer

Kosher salt, to taste

1 tablespoon chives, minced

Zest of 1 orange

2 quarts vegetable oil, for frying

1½ pounds cod, cut into small pieces for kids and larger ones for adults

Lemon wedges, to serve

Malt vinegar, to serve

Potato chips, to serve

1. In a medium bowl, stir together the flour, baking powder, baking soda, and cornstarch.

2. In a large bowl, beat together the eggs and milk. Whisk in the beer. Stir this wet mixture into the flour mixture. Season with salt and add the chives and orange zest.

3. In an electric deep fryer or a heavy saucepan, heat the oil to 360 °F.

4. Season the fish liberally with salt and dust with flour. Coat the fish in batter, and submerge in the hot oil. Fry in batches until golden brown, about 4–5 minutes.

5. Remove the fish to a paper towel–lined plate and season with a little more salt. Serve with lemon wedges, malt vinegar, and potato chips

Dry and wet

For smooth, lumpless batter, mix your wet ingredients first and then add to the dry ingredients. This works for all batters, including pancakes. And speaking of dry, make sure to pat the fish dry before battering.

Frying: the golden rule

Fry only until the crust turns light golden, not dark brown. When it does, immediately drain on paper towels and season with salt.

Size matters

For kids and other picky eaters, I recommend making the fillet pieces small enough to pick up with a toothpick (although you are allowed to use a fork if you like). The point is, if it's just a mouthful, people are more willing to try it, and once they've had that first moist, crunchy, flaky piece, the sale is made. They'll be back for more. Count on it.

MOM'S CHICKEN WITH SAFFRON, OLIVES, AND ONIONS

SERVES 6 | **Skill Level: EASY** | **Cook Time: 40–45 mins.** | **Prep Time: 15 mins.** | **Cost: $$**

"My mom used to make . . ." That's a phrase we all use, and for each of us it brings up the strongest and often the most pleasant memories. You may forget who was the king of England in 1602, or where Columbus set sail from, but no one forgets their mom's pancakes, or meatloaf, or, in the case of this recipe, my mother's chicken with saffron. She made it all the time when we were in junior high and high school. I can literally taste and smell that dish just by saying the words. It's not very demanding. It just requires patience. Let your onions caramelize over low heat for a good long while. Then when you add liquid, it's just a little at a time. You want a good thick broth, not a thin soupy gravy.

8 chicken thighs

Kosher salt, to taste

Cayenne pepper, to taste

2 tablespoons extra virgin olive oil

4 yellow onions, thinly sliced

1 tablespoon all-purpose flour

½ cup chicken stock

1 teaspoon saffron

2 bay leaves

½ cup pitted Moroccan olives

3 tablespoons cilantro, minced, for garnish

1 scallion, chopped, for garnish

1 pomegranate, separated into seeds, for garnish

1. Season the chicken pieces with salt and cayenne.

2. Heat a large Dutch oven over medium-high heat and add the oil. When the oil is hot, add the chicken and brown, cooking for 4–6 minutes on each side. Remove the chicken to a plate and set aside.

3. Add the onions and cook for another 8–10 minutes, until soft and browned. Stir in the flour and season again with salt and cayenne, depending on how hot you like it.

4. Stir in the chicken stock, and add the chicken pieces back to the pan. Top with the saffron, bay leaves, and olives.

5. Bring to a simmer, cover, and reduce the heat to medium. Stir occasionally and cook for about 20–25 minutes, or until the chicken is tender.

6. Serve on a large platter and finish with chopped cilantro and scallions, and sprinkle with pomegranate seeds.

BIG TURKEY MEATBALL SUBS

SERVES 6 | Skill Level: EASY | Cook Time: 35 mins. | Prep Time: 25 mins. | Cost: $

The secret to making great meatballs isn't necessarily the meat. Let's take it for granted that you start with a mound of beautiful ground meat, not too lean (or you will end up with something that's chewy, rubbery, and no fun). It's what you mix it with that makes all the difference. In this case, I start with a mix of turkey and sausage and then I add in some freshly grated Pecorino cheese, eggs, crunchy bread crumbs, and milk. Then—very important—mix thoroughly. What does thoroughly mean? When you think it is mixed enough, give it another 10 seconds. The result is a meatball that holds its shape but is tender and moist. This is one of those recipes that's ideal for a potluck meal because all that needs to be done is reheat. No on-site fussing required.

2 cups panko bread crumbs

1½–2 cups milk

2 pounds ground turkey

4 ounces prosciutto di Parma, cut into ⅛-inch dice

8 ounces sweet Italian sausage, casings removed

3 large eggs

½ cup freshly grated Pecorino Romano

¼ cup freshly grated Parmigiano-Reggiano

¾ cup Italian parsley, finely chopped

Several gratings of nutmeg

½ cup extra virgin olive oil

Salt

Freshly ground black pepper

2 cups Mario's Basic Tomato Sauce (see page 30)

6 soft Italian rolls

12 slices provolone cheese

1. Soak the bread crumbs in the milk for 5 minutes. Strain out the bread crumbs and set aside, reserving the milk.

2. In a large bowl, combine the turkey, prosciutto, sausage, bread crumbs, eggs, reserved milk, ¼ cup of the Pecorino, the Parmigiano, ½ cup of the parsley, the nutmeg, and ¼ cup of the olive oil, and mix very gently with your hands. Season with salt and pepper.

3. Form the mixture into 1 ½ -inch balls and set aside.

4. Add the tomato sauce to a pan and bring to a boil. Place the meatballs in the sauce and return to a boil, then lower the heat and simmer for 30 minutes.

5. Lay 2 slices of provolone in each roll and top with 3 or 4 meatballs. Garnish with the remaining Pecorino and parsley sprinkled over the top.

SPRING

143

Entertaining with Pizzazz

HAVE YOU EVER DECIDED to throw a party and got that icky feeling inside like you don't want to throw this party anymore because it's going to cost too much? And that's before you buy the drinks? I've got five easy and inexpensive tabletop ideas where you save money by doing it yourself.

Who needs tablecloths?

The bummer about tablecloths is they can really be an expensive number and you've got to be satisfied with what the designers want you to have. You can express yourself and save your wallet if you go to the fabric store and buy some fabric by the yard. It ranges anywhere from five to twenty dollars per yard.

Okay, I can hear you saying, "What about those nasty frayed edges?"

And I answer, "Hey, you're getting a bargain, don't complain." Some iron-on tape makes for a fast and easy hem that will last through anything, except maybe a toga party. While you're shopping, keep an eye out for smaller remnants. They make great one-of-a-kind placemats and runners.

Color scheming

Now that you have your tablecloth, think like a designer. How will the rest of your décor pick up on the color theme? Suppose you have a checked tablecloth with a lot of blue in it. It's telling you something.

Now grab some wine bottles from the recycle bin, clean off the labels, and then spray-paint them blue. Voilà! You now have custom-colored candleholders that give a coordinated look to your room. I find that high-gloss paint gives some extra sparkle and reflects the light of the candles.

Mirror magic

The next time you go to a yard sale, keep your eyes open for antique mirrors. Clean them up and they make great trays for hors d'oeuvres, cheeses, and fruits. It adds some sparkle, shine, and romance to a table setting, especially with the candles.

Gourd-geous

I can hear your groans at my pun even as I write. I'm talking about gourds—dried squashes. People have been using them as table décor forever, and they'll get no argument from me, but if you spray-paint them a high-gloss black (again to reflect light), then you have these knobby odd-shaped weird things that look interesting on the serving table.

Make a new friend

Flowers make everyone happy. *Make friends with your local florist.* Then drop by at the end of the day and see if you can have the castaways—the blooms that might not make it through tomorrow. They'll be just fine for your party and won't cost a stem and a leg. I wouldn't worry too much about the fine points of flower arranging. I don't. The flowers themselves are beautiful to begin with, so stick them in a bunch of little vases and Mother Nature will be the best decorator's assistant you ever had.

The Chew crew celebrates Mama T's birthday.

PAELLA

SERVES 8 | Skill Level: EASY | Cook Time: 40–45 mins. | Prep Time: 15 mins. | Cost: $$

Paella is one of those words that might as well have a blinking light and sound effects coming off the page. Like a burger, or pizza, or cappuccino, it makes me feel good. When you use the best fresh seafood, succulent dark meat chicken, and savory sausage, you've got my attention. The ability of rice to suck up and marry those flavors is what makes paella so comforting and satisfying. I always caution people that making paella is not like making risotto. When you make risotto, you are looking for ultimate creaminess in the rice, constantly stirring as it cooks. With paella, although you get some creaminess, if you don't bother it too much while it's cooking and let it work its magic, you get a beautiful crunchy crust called socarrat. *Flavorful crunch is always a crowd pleaser. Just watch what your kids go for when you put anything with crunch in front of them.*

1 tablespoon olive oil

½ pound Spanish chorizo

8 chicken thighs

Salt, to taste

Freshly ground black pepper, to taste

1 yellow onion, chopped

2 cups short-grain rice

¼ cup white wine

1 heaping teaspoon saffron threads

1½ cups San Marzano tomatoes, drained and chopped

5 cups chicken stock

12 mussels, debearded and scrubbed

12 littleneck clams, scrubbed

1 pound large shrimp

1 cup frozen peas

¼ cup flat-leaf parsley, chopped, for garnish

1. Preheat the oven to 350 °F.

2. In a paella pan or a large high-sided skillet, heat the olive oil over medium heat. Add the chorizo and cook until it has browned and rendered some of its fat, about 3 minutes. Remove the chorizo from the pan and set aside on a plate.

3. Season the chicken with salt and pepper and add to the pan, browning for 3–4 minutes per side. Remove to the plate with the chorizo.

4. Add the onion and cook until translucent, about 5 minutes.

5. Add the rice and toast, stirring to coat the rice in the oil. Deglaze the pan with the white wine and add the saffron and the chopped tomatoes.

6. Slowly add the stock, stirring as you add. Season again with salt, and add the chicken and chorizo back to the pan. Nestle the mussels, clams, and shrimp into the rice. Sprinkle the peas all around and cover with foil and place in the oven.

7. Cook for 25–30 minutes, or until the clams and mussels have opened and the chicken has cooked through. Remove from the oven and take straight to the table. Garnish with chopped parsley and enjoy.

Saffronific

Saffron is pretty pricey. But when you realize that it takes more than 100,000 crocus blossoms to make a pound—and they are all picked by hand—then you can understand the price. Still, a little goes a very long way. A pinch of saffron only costs a couple of dollars and it makes a big difference in flavor. Go for it!

CURRIED CHICKEN AND DUMPLINGS

| SERVES 6 | Skill Level: EASY | Cook Time: 25–30 mins. | Prep Time: 20 mins. | Cost: $ |

Look in any American recipe book from the last 150 years and you are going to find some version of curried chicken and some form of chicken and dumplings. I think they're telling us something: these are two great ways to make chicken, which I have combined here into one super chicken recipe. One of the things I love about it is that once you've bought the chicken, you probably have everything else in your pantry and your vegetable drawer. I mean, who doesn't have a can of chicken broth on the shelf? And I'm willing to bet that you have a tin of curry powder that's been hanging around your spice shelf since 1776. And if you are like me, then you probably have some coconut milk too. If you don't, get some. It's so good in so many ways.

FOR THE CHICKEN:

2 tablespoons olive oil

1 cup all-purpose flour, for dusting

Salt, to taste

Pepper, to taste

6 boneless, skinless chicken thighs

1 onion, diced

3 stalks celery, diced

3 carrots, diced

2 tablespoons curry powder

½ teaspoon cayenne pepper

4 cups chicken stock

1 12-ounce can coconut milk

1 cup cooked chickpeas

FOR THE DUMPLINGS:

1½ cups chickpea flour

¼ cup all-purpose flour

½ teaspoon salt

1 teaspoon baking soda

1 cup Greek yogurt

¼ cup fresh parsley, chopped

¼ cup fresh cilantro, chopped

1. Preheat the oven to 350 °F.

2. Heat the olive oil in a Dutch oven. Season the flour with salt and pepper, and dredge the chicken in the flour, shaking off any excess. Add the chicken to the pan and brown on both sides, about 2 minutes per side. Remove the chicken to a plate and set aside.

3. Add the onion, celery, and carrots to the pot, and cook for 3 minutes. Stir in the curry powder and cayenne pepper.

4. Add the chicken broth, coconut milk, chickpeas, and browned chicken, and bring to a simmer.

5. Place the dumpling ingredients in a mixing bowl and stir until combined.

6. Dollop tablespoons of the dumpling mixture into the pot.

7. Place into the oven uncovered for 15–20 minutes, or until the dumplings are golden brown and cooked through.

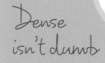

Dense isn't dumb

Coconut milk is what food scientists call "nutrient dense": it's full of things that are good for you, particularly protein. I love it in fish stews with poultry, and it's an interesting, flavorful base for stewing vegetables.

GREEK EASTER LEG OF LAMB

SERVES 12 | Skill Level: **EASY** | Cook Time: 1½–2 hrs. | Prep Time: 20 mins. | Cost: $

Inactive Prep Time: 24 hrs.

A lot of our viewers Twittered and Facebooked us asking how to make lamb for Easter. Being of Greek heritage, I thought lamb on this happy and holy day was the 11th Commandment. We always made a whole lamb on a spit. We'd baste it with lemon and oregano and olive oil. It was amazing!!! It's also something that most folks aren't going to tackle at home, so here is a leg of lamb recipe that I think delivers a lot of the flavor and texture of my family's Easter lamb.

Apart from having a great piece of meat, using an herb and spice rub that sits on the lamb for 24 hours or at least overnight raises the level of flavor to the peak of Mt. Olympus.

FOR THE ROASTED LAMB:

6 shallots, minced

4 cloves garlic, minced

¼ cup fresh rosemary

¼ cup fresh oregano

2 tablespoons sugar

2 tablespoons coriander seeds, toasted and crushed

1 tablespoon crushed red pepper flakes

1½ tablespoons kosher salt

1 6-pound bone-in leg of lamb

Rosemary sprigs (optional)

3 tablespoons olive oil

TO MAKE THE ROASTED LAMB:

1. Mix together in a medium bowl the shallots, garlic, spices, and herbs. Rub the mixture all over the surface of the lamb. Place in a large glass baking dish, cover with plastic wrap, and refrigerate overnight. Remove the lamb from the baking dish, rinse off the seasonings, and pat dry. Let the lamb sit at room temperature for 1 hour. Preheat the oven to 375 °F.

2. Heat a roasting pan or large ovenproof skillet over medium heat. Add olive oil and heat until it begins to smoke and then add the lamb and brown on all sides, 7–10 minutes. Transfer the lamb, fat side up, to a roasting rack set into a roasting pan. If you have extra rosemary, lay the sprigs over the lamb with a drizzle of olive oil over the top. Roast until the lamb reaches an internal temperature of 140 °F, about 1½ hours.

3. Remove the lamb from the pan and set it aside to rest for 20 minutes.

4. Slice and serve with the tzatziki sauce and roasted potatoes.

FOR THE ROASTED POTATOES:

4 pounds unpeeled fingerling potatoes, rinsed and halved lengthwise

½ cup olive oil

Salt

Freshly ground black pepper

1 cup extra virgin olive oil

½ cup fresh lemon juice

6 tablespoons fresh dill, chopped

4 teaspoons lemon peel, finely grated

24 cloves garlic, sliced

FOR THE TZATZIKI SAUCE:

2 cups Greek yogurt

1 cucumber

Kosher salt, to taste

Juice and zest of 2 lemons

2 tablespoons fresh mint, chopped

1 tablespoon garlic, minced

1 tablespoon shallot, minced

Freshly ground black pepper, to taste

TO MAKE THE POTATOES:

5. Position a rack in the top third and a rack in the bottom third of the oven, and preheat to 375 °F. Spray two large-rimmed baking sheets with nonstick spray. Toss the potatoes with ½ cup olive oil in a large bowl. Sprinkle generously with salt and freshly ground black pepper. Spread the potatoes in a single layer on the baking sheets, dividing equally. Roast 30 minutes, tossing the potatoes halfway through.

6. Meanwhile, whisk the extra virgin olive oil, lemon juice, dill, and lemon peel in a small bowl to blend for dressing. Toss the garlic and 2 tablespoons dressing in another small bowl. Divide the garlic mixture between the baking sheets and toss with the potatoes; reverse the baking sheets and continue to roast until the potatoes are tender and brown around the edges, about 15 minutes longer.

7. Toss the roasted potatoes in a large bowl with the remaining dressing to coat and serve.

TO MAKE THE TZATZIKI SAUCE:

8. Put the yogurt in a cheesecloth-lined strainer set over a bowl and let drain for 24 hours in the refrigerator. Peel and dice the cucumber, sprinkle it with salt, and place in a strainer at room temperature for 2–3 hours to drain.

9. Stir together the yogurt, cucumber, lemon juice and zest, mint, garlic, and shallot in a medium bowl until thoroughly combined. Season to taste with salt and pepper.

Great on the grill too

Grilling the lamb on a charcoal grill is a way to get wood fire crustiness that pumps up the flavor even more. With big pieces of meat like this, you want a hot fire in one part of the grill and a very low one in the other. You start out by searing the meat all over on the hot side of the grill and then, to finish cooking, move it over to the cooler side, covering it and fiddling with the coals and the vents to keep the heat at about 350 °F.

POT ROAST WITH SHAVED CARROT SALAD

| SERVES 8 | Skill Level: EASY | Cook Time: 2–2½ hrs. | Prep Time: 20 mins. | Cost: $ |

Here we have comfort food that reflects my M&M roots—that stands for Mediterranean and Midwestern. A beautifully browned pot roast is the Mediterranean part. The crunchy, tangy carrot salad that cuts through the big, strong meaty flavor is the kind of taste and flavor matchup we love in the Midwest. Braised in beer and apple cider, and given some extra meaty oomph from bacon, it brings back memories of cool spring days when the hills are finally shaking off their winter coat and the first hints of green brighten the Ohio countryside.

FOR THE POT ROAST:

3 tablespoons extra virgin olive oil

1 3-pound brisket

Salt, to taste

Pepper, to taste

2 tablespoons coriander, toasted and crushed

½ pound bacon, diced

1 red onion, sliced

2 cloves garlic, smashed

2 carrots, peeled and roughly chopped

1 jalapeño, split

1 12-ounce bottle beer

1½–2 cups water

12 ounces apple cider

FOR THE SALAD:

4 carrots, shaved

1 bunch mint leaves

1 bunch scallions, sliced

2 tablespoons red wine vinegar

3 tablespoons olive oil

Salt, to taste

Pepper, to taste

1. Preheat the oven to 325 °F.

2. Heat a large Dutch oven over medium-high heat and add the olive oil. When hot, season the brisket with salt, pepper, and coriander and add to the pan. Sear on both sides until brown, about 3 minutes per side. Remove the brisket to a large plate and add the bacon to the pan. Cook the bacon until crispy, about 5 minutes. Once cooked, remove from pan and set aside.

3. Add the onion, garlic, carrots, and jalapeño pepper to the pan, and sauté until tender, about 3 more minutes. Season with salt and pepper. Stir in beer, water, and the apple cider. Add the brisket and the bacon back to the pan. Bring to a boil, cover, and place into the oven. Cook the brisket for 2–2½ hours at 325 °F, until tender.

4. For the salad, place the carrots, mint, and scallions in a large bowl with the vinegar. Season with salt and pepper and toss to coat. Drizzle in the olive oil and toss.

5. Slice the brisket and serve with the carrot salad. Use any leftover brisket to make Bahn Mi (see page 153).

BAHN MI

SERVES 4 TO 6, depending on the amount of leftovers │ Skill Level: EASY │ Cook Time: 20 mins.

Prep Time: 20 mins. │ COST: $

Whenever you make a brisket or a pot roast, you are pretty much guaranteed that there will be leftovers. If you want something more exciting than reheating in the microwave, these sliders make for a completely new and delicious use of yesterday's beef.

Leftover pot roast from Pot Roast with Shaved Carrot Salad (see page 152)

FOR THE PICKLES:

1 cup rice wine vinegar

2 tablespoons sugar

1 bunch radishes, thinly sliced

2 carrots, julienned

FOR THE CHILI MAYO:

½ cup mayonnaise

1 tablespoon Sriracha

8–16 soft slider buns, to serve

1 English cucumber, thinly sliced, to serve

1 bunch cilantro leaves, to serve

1 bunch mint leaves, to garnish

2 scallions, sliced on the bias, to garnish

1. Place the leftover brisket and all of its juices into a baking dish and back into the oven at 350 °F until warmed through, about 20 minutes.

2. For the pickles, heat the vinegar and sugar together until the sugar is dissolved, and pour over the radishes and carrots. Set aside to cool. Meanwhile, combine the mayonnaise and Sriracha and set aside.

3. To serve, place some of the shredded brisket on the bottom half of a bun, and top with pickles, cucumber, and cilantro. Spread some of the mayo on the other half of the bun and top. Garnish with the mint and scallions.

Get down with brown

A lot of people think that when you brown the outside of a piece of meat, you are "sealing in the juices," but scientists tell us that you are not really sealing in anything. What you are doing, though, is one of the most wonderful things in cuisine. They call it the Maillard Reaction, and it's responsible for that brown crust full of beautiful flavors that you get when you take the time to get the meat good and brown over high heat. Don't be shy here. We're talking brown, not a light tan.

RED VELVET CAKE

SERVES 12 | **Skill Level: EASY** | **Cook Time: 1½ hrs.** | **Prep Time: 20 mins.** | **Cost: $**

Who doesn't like winning an election? I sure was happy when viewers were asked to vote for a favorite recipe, because my Red Velvet Cake came in first! That's saying something when you consider the runners-up were hush puppies and waffles, which are two of my favorites. Hey, I'm a southern girl, and the southern part will always love her hush puppies, while the girl in me remembers waffles so fondly. People say this is a sexy cake (Clinton does, but he says that about everything except maybe boiled turnips). The color red no doubt has a lot to do with its sexy reputation: think Valentine's Day. This is a fun cake to make with kids, and I guarantee that after eating this cake, most kids will be happy to have learned that beets aren't yucky!

FOR THE CAKE:

Butter, for the cake pans

2½ cups all-purpose flour, plus more for the cake pans

1½ cups sugar

1 teaspoon baking soda

1 teaspoon salt

2 tablespoons cocoa powder

½ cup vegetable oil

¾ cup buttermilk

½ cup roasted beet puree (recipe follows)

2 eggs at room temperature

2 tablespoons red food coloring

1 teaspoon white vinegar

1 teaspoon vanilla extract

FOR THE FROSTING:

16 ounces cream cheese at room temperature

1 stick butter at room temperature

2 cups white chocolate chips, melted

1 teaspoon vanilla

2 cups powdered sugar

1. Place 2 large red beets in a piece of foil and season with salt. Top with olive oil and a splash of water and roast in the oven until a knife or skewer comes out with ease when inserted into the beet. This should take around 25–30 minutes. Remove the beets and set aside to cool just enough to handle. Peel the beets and place into a blender with any remaining juices and puree.

2. Preheat oven to 350 °F. Butter and flour two 9-inch round cake pans. Line with parchment. In the bowl of a standing mixer, combine the dry ingredients. Mix for 30 seconds with a paddle attachment.

3. In a separate bowl, combine the wet ingredients. In two parts, pour the wet ingredients into the mixer. Mix on medium speed until combined. Do not overmix. Pour the batter into the prepared pans. Bake on the center rack for 35 minutes or until a toothpick inserted in the center comes out clean. Cool for 10 minutes, then turn out on a wire rack. Cool cakes completely.

4. Meanwhile, beat the cream cheese and butter in a large bowl with an electric mixer until combined. Add the melted chocolate and vanilla, and then continue to mix until incorporated. Next, slowly add the sugar, beating until the frosting is light and fluffy.

FOR THE ROASTED BEET PUREE:

2 large beets

¼ teaspoon salt

1 tablespoon olive oil

splash of water

5. Cut each cake in half horizontally to make four layers. Frost the top of each layer, then sides, finishing with the top.

SEBADAS

SERVES 8 | Skill Level: MODERATE | Cook Time: 15 mins. | Prep Time: 30 mins. | Cost: $

Inactive Prep Time: 1 hr.

Sebadas are fried raviolis with a sweet stuffing: just imagining that combo makes you want to pick up your fork. I make sebadas on the sweet side as a dessert, but in Sardinia, where the sebada originated, it was originally served as a savory course. Depending on how much honey you use, you can go either way, but I love them best as a dessert fritter. Chestnut honey, if you can find it, has a nutty, floral perfume that pairs up magically with fresh ricotta and yogurt. If you have a farmers' market nearby, pick up some fresh goat's milk yogurt.

Turn the page and see Daphne's healthier version. At least she says it's healthier. I think it's just the difference between her Turkish ancestors and my Italian peeps.

2 cups sheep's milk ricotta

Zest of 2 lemons

1 egg

1 cup yogurt

¼ cup sugar

1 cup all-purpose flour

½ cup bench flour

1 cup superfine semolina

½ cup warm milk

4 ounces butter, softened

2 cups olive oil

Powdered sugar, to garnish

1 cup chestnut honey, to serve

1. In a mixing bowl, stir together the ricotta, lemon zest, egg, yogurt, and sugar until well blended.

2. In another mixing bowl, place both flours and the semolina in a well.

3. In a small saucepan, stir together the milk and butter until butter is melted. Pour into the well of flour and incorporate wet into dry to form a dough. Knead the dough for 1 minute, form a ball, then wrap and refrigerate for 1 hour.

4. In a 12- to 14-inch frying pan, heat the oil to 375 °F.

5. With a pasta roller, roll out the pastry to ¼ inch thick. Cut 20 3½-inch rounds out of the pastry. Place 2 tablespoons cheese mixture on 10 rounds, and cover each like a sandwich. Press the edges together to seal, and fry in the oil until golden brown, about 1 minute. Remove and drain on paper towels.

6. Sprinkle with powdered sugar and serve with warm honey.

SWEET PHYLLO PACKETS

SERVES 8 | **Skill Level: EASY** | **Cook Time: 15 mins.** | **Prep Time: 15 mins.** | **Cost: $**

All of us on The Chew—and that includes the crew and the audience—really love Mario's Sebadas. Here's a version with less calories from fat, white flour, and sugar. I realize that you're not going to make a pastry with no fat, no flour, and no sweetener: Why bother? The big difference here is Mario's recipe has a rich filling in a heavy dough, while I make a slightly less sweetened ricotta filling inside of wafer-thin phyllo dough, and then I bake instead of frying. You're always cutting down on calories from fat when you bake instead of fry. If you count calories, mine have 600 calories less. If you can get true dessert satisfaction with fewer calories, it's definitely worth thinking about.

2 cups sheep's milk ricotta

1 egg

2 tablespoons honey

1 teaspoon vanilla

Pinch of salt

1 package phyllo dough, thawed

4 ounces butter, melted

1. Preheat the oven to 350 °F.

2. In a mixing bowl, stir together the ricotta, egg, honey, vanilla, and salt until well blended.

3. Lay out the phyllo sheets, two at a time, with the shortest side closest to you, and brush with butter. Cut the phyllo vertically into three equal pieces. Place 2 tablespoons of the mixture at the end closest to you, and fold the corner upward to make a triangle. Continue folding all the way up (you should have a triangular packet).

4. Place the packet on a sheet pan and brush with a little more butter. Once all of the packets are made, place the sheet pan into the oven and cook until golden brown, about 15 minutes. Remove from the oven and transfer to a platter. Drizzle a little extra honey over the packets.

Agave—sweeter than sugar

If honey isn't your cup of tea, try some agave sugar: nectar is made from the heart of the agave cactus, which is the same plant that provides the raw material for tequila. Ounce for ounce, it is sweeter than table sugar and vegans often use it as a substitute for honey. I like it because it's all natural. If you keep track of such things, it has a lower glycemic index than many sweeteners, so it spikes your blood sugar less than refined sugar. Still, even without resorting to a long chart, you want to be mindful of how much sugar of any kind you consume.

COCONUT PECAN POUND CAKE

SERVES 8 to 10 | Skill Level: EASY | Cook Time: 1 hr. 10 mins. | Prep Time: 10 mins. | Cost: $

For pure knockout flavor, nothing on this whole planet gets my vote like this cake. My grandmother made it every year at Christmas. I do the same. It is worth every calorie—and there are plenty of them, so don't make it every day as my Chew family took great delight in pointing out:

Clinton said, "When you give this as a gift, you're basically saying, 'Here's 5 pounds right on the belly.'"

And Michael chimed in, "You may think you're giving the gift of love, but what you are really giving is a gym membership."

Oh, well, I guess it was National Pile on the Health Guru Day. I don't mind. If you can't tease your family, then who can you tease? I look at this cake as a gift of love. How many gifts do you give that end up cluttering the closet a year later? This one gets eaten in a day. It rings all the bells: it's appreciated, it brings back warm memories of childhood, and—here's the kicker—it's eighty-five cents a serving.

FOR THE CAKE:

2 cups sugar

1 cup unsalted butter

4 eggs

3 cups flour

½ teaspoon baking powder

½ teaspoon salt

1 cup buttermilk

1 cup unsweetened flaked coconut

1 cup pecans, chopped

FOR THE GLAZE:

½ cup water

2 tablespoons salted butter

1 cup sugar

Powdered sugar, for dusting

TO MAKE THE CAKE:

1. Preheat the oven to 350 °F.

2. In a large bowl, combine the sugar and butter and beat with an electric mixer until light and fluffy, approximately 3 minutes. Add in the eggs one at a time, until combined.

3. Combine the flour, baking powder, and salt in a separate bowl.

4. Add the dry ingredients, alternating with the buttermilk, in three parts to the batter and mix gently, until just moistened. Stir in the coconut and pecans. Pour the batter into a pound cake mold. Bake for 60 minutes, or until a knife inserted in the center comes out clean.

TO MAKE THE GLAZE:

5. Five minutes before the cake is finished baking, make the glaze. Combine the water, butter, and sugar in a saucepan, and bring to a boil. Reduce heat and cook for 5 minutes.

6. Slowly pour half the syrup over the cake, invert the cake onto a serving plate, and pour the remaining syrup over the top. Dust with powdered sugar. Let sit for 10 minutes, and eat warm!

SPRING

BANANA PUDDIN

SERVES 6 | Skill Level: EASY | Cook Time: 10 mins. | Prep Time: 10 mins. | Cost: $

Inactive Cook Time: 2 hrs.

If you're from the South and you've been to a church supper, or a barbecue, or a tailgate, then you have had banana puddin. That's not a spelling error. I was almost a grown woman before I realized there is a g at the end of pudding. That's the way we talk where I come from. No recipe could be easier or creamier . . . or yummier. The classic calls for vanilla wafers, but I often use shortbread, which is even richer. I also like to give mine a little kick with some rum.

1 cup sugar

⅛ teaspoon salt

⅓ cup all-purpose flour

2 cups milk (low fat or whole)

2 eggs, separated

2 bananas, very ripe and mashed, plus 2 bananas, ripe but firm, sliced

2 tablespoons butter, softened

1½ teaspoons vanilla

About 44 small vanilla shortbread cookies

2 cups whipped cream

1 teaspoon rum

Zest of 1 lemon

1. Combine ¾ cup granulated sugar, salt, and flour in a medium bowl. Slowly stir milk into dry mixture.

2. Put the mixture on top of a double boiler over simmering water, and cook until the mixture begins to thicken, about 5 minutes.

3. Beat the egg yolks and mashed bananas in a small bowl, then briskly stir a small amount of the hot milk mixture (about ½ cup).

4. Add the egg-milk mixture into the hot mixture on top of the double boiler, and stir in the butter and vanilla. Cook until mixture thickens again, about 5 more minutes.

5. Place a layer of vanilla shortbread cookies in an 11-by-7-inch baking dish (or any other shape 2-quart shallow baking dish). Add a layer of sliced bananas. Continue layering until all the cookies and banana slices are used. Pour the pudding mixture over top, and place in the refrigerator to cool (at least 2 hours, and up to overnight).

6. When cooled completely and ready to serve, in a bowl, whip the remaining ¼ cup sugar into the heavy cream. Mix in the rum and lemon zest, and whip until soft peaks form. Top the pudding with whipped cream.

Temper, temper

It is so important that you temper the eggs when you add in the hot flour, sugar, and milk mixture. Think about getting into a hot tub. You'd never jump right in. You'd dip your toe and then slowly work your way in. It's the same idea when you temper ingredients. Take your time. With Banana Puddin, this means that you gradually warm the eggs so that they don't scramble and separate from the other ingredients. An easy way to do this is to slowly add the hot milk mixture to the eggs and bananas. When the bowl starts to feel warm, the eggs are tempered and you can go ahead and combine the rest of the hot milk mixture with the rest of the ingredients.

MINT JULEP

SERVES 1 | Skill Level: EASY | Cook Time: 10 mins. | Prep Time: 5 mins. | Cost: $

This is the traditional cocktail that they serve at the Kentucky Derby. It's a great drink to usher in spring and summer: a beautiful horse race, people in their warm weather finery, and a cold, delicious glassful of good cheer. If you can't make it to the Derby, it's perfect at a slightly fancy backyard party. Most of the time when people come over for a barbecue, they're wearing their plaid shorts and a wifebeater. Sometimes it's just nice to say on an invitation: "A slightly fancy barbecue."

Crushed ice

2 ounces bourbon

1 ounce simple syrup (recipe follows)

1 slice sugar cane (optional)

2–3 sprigs mint, to garnish

1. Place the ice in a glass and top with the bourbon and the simple syrup. Stir with the sugar cane and garnish with mint.

MINT SIMPLE SYRUP

1 cup water

1 cup sugar

½ bunch mint (leaves only)

2. Heat the water and sugar in a small saucepan over medium heat until the sugar dissolves, about 10 minutes. Remove from the heat and add the mint leaves. Steep for 3-4 minutes, and then strain and refrigerate.

STRAWBERRY WHITE WINE COOLER PUNCH

SERVES 6 | **Skill Level: EASY** | **Prep time: 15 mins.** | **Cost: $**

The 1980s brought many memorable things: the "Thriller" video, Miami Vice, and, of course, Big Hair, but nothing better than wine coolers. The ones that came in a box were a nice way to charge five bucks for fifty cents' worth of ingredients. I find you can do a whole lot better cost-wise and flavor-wise if you make your own. When she tried this, even Miss I'm-Not-Into-Alcohol Carla said, "Oh, I love it!"

2 cups strawberries, plus extra for garnish

⅓ cup sugar

1 bottle of dry white wine

Crushed ice

Ginger ale

1. In a bowl, combine the strawberries and sugar and let sit for 10 minutes. In a blender, puree the strawberry mixture with wine until smooth and pour through a fine sieve into a pitcher.

2. Wine cooler may be made 4 hours ahead and refrigerated. Serve chilled over ice, and top with ginger ale and strawberries.

Luke Mangan joins the crew in some Easter Funday laughs.

The CHEW

RHUBARB PUNCH

SERVES 10 | **Skill Level: EASY** | **Cook Time: 10 mins.** | **Prep time: 10 mins.** | **Cost: $**

One of my favorite times of the year is late spring when the roses are in bloom, the strawberries are dark red, and pucker-your-mouth rhubarb is in season. I don't know where rhubarb would find a place in life if it didn't go so well with strawberries. It just goes to show you that it's important to have a good side-kick—in life and in your glass. So fire up the grill for the first barbecue of the year, and while you're waiting for the coals to reach perfection, kick back with this tangy, fizzy drink. This recipe doesn't call for any alcohol. I suppose you could add some gin, or vodka, or tequila, but it's nice to have a special, fun drink for the teetotalers in the crowd (like me).

8 cups fresh rhubarb, chopped

2½ cups sugar

2 cups pineapple juice

¼ cup lime juice

1 pint strawberries, hulled and chilled

6 cups ginger ale

1. In a Dutch oven, bring the rhubarb and 2 quarts water to a boil. Reduce heat and simmer, uncovered, for 10 minutes. Strain, reserving liquid.

2. In a large bowl, dissolve the sugar in 2 cups boiling water. Stir in the pineapple and lime juices. Stir in the reserved rhubarb liquid and refrigerate until chilled.

3. Just before serving, pour into a punch bowl, add the strawberries, and stir in the ginger ale.

SUMMER

WATERMELON GAZPACHO, 172 | WHITE GAZPACHO WITH FROZEN GRAPES, 174 | GRILLED VEGETABLE AND PEACH SUMMER SALAD, 175 | SWEET CORN WITH ONIONS AND BASIL, 176 | SUMMER SCAFATA, 177 | GRILLED EGGPLANT WITH GREEK YOGURT, 179 | DAPHNE'S SUPERFOODS SMOOTHIE, 180 | MUSSELS ALLA PIASTRA, 181 | FRIED CLAM SANDWICH, 182 | MICHAEL SYMON'S TWICE-FRIED CHICKEN, 185 | GRANDMA THELMA'S FRIED CHICKEN, 186 | FETTUCCINE WITH LOBSTER, TOMATOES, AND SAFFRON, 187 | CORN DOGGIN', 188 | BIG MIKE BURGER, 189 | CHEESE-STUFFED MORTADELLA ON BRUSCHETTA, 195 | TURKEY SLIDERS, 196 | DAPHNE'S BEST BURGER, 198 | DRY RUB BABY BACK RIBS WITH SCALLOPED POTATOES, 200 | T-BONE FIORENTINA, 202 | BLUEBERRY HAND PIES, 204 | PEACH COBBLER, 207 | ZOMBIE, 208 | WHITE SANGRIA, 211 | FROZEN FRUIT SORBET, 212

A gluten-free pork dish satisfies both Michael and Elisabeth Hasselbeck.

Q&A WITH

Michael

Q: **What makes cooking on *The Chew* special for you?**

Michael: I love a live audience, I love to watch it, I love to do it, because you can see the mistakes. Take it from someone who's worked and run restaurants for over 25 years, mistakes happen . . . in my restaurant and in my home. It's your ability to be able to fix them that makes you a good cook. And I think that's what someone like Julia Child used to bring to us. She'd make a mistake, she'd do something to fix the mistake, and it was okay. After Julia, what happened with cooking on television is what I call the Martha effect; everything got so perfect but wasn't necessarily real or attainable. If a viewer made something that didn't look exactly like it did on the cooking show, they thought that they were a bad cook, got discouraged. And in reality, that's life in a nutshell: sometimes the dish doesn't look perfect, but it doesn't mean it's any less delicious. That's what people learn when they see a show like this.

Q: **Does that mean cooking on *The Chew* is oversimplified or dumbed down?**

Michael: No way. The cool thing about *The Chew* is it's not dumbed down at all. Most of the stuff is made on the show without dump and stir. One of the things that makes it approachable is the comradeship among the five of us. I loved doing *Iron Chef* and I'm proud that I could do that show very well. But is that how I cook at home, for friends and family? Absolutely not! Food should bring people together. It should be delicious. It should be nourishing. And it should make people happy.

Q: **When you guys came on the show, you fit certain roles. How did you see yours?**

Michael: Heartland food is what I like talking about because that's how I was raised. No matter how much you evolve as a TV host or chef or whatever, there's always going to be a pocket for you that's most comfortable. And the heartland has always been my pocket.

Q: **Clinton was hired for his hosting chops and his Mister Mingle personality, but he's a pretty good cook, isn't he?**

Michael: I knew instantly when I met him how much he loved food. But there's a lot of people in the world that can cook, and there are a lot of people that can host. There are very few people who can cook *and* host. He does both very, very well. He's very comfortable in the kitchen. He thinks about the dishes and he's a great entertainer.

Q: **Are there any mistakes that have happened on the show that are really memorable?**

Michael: Oh, yeah, I mean the one that's most memorable and obvious for me is I worked with a woman in the audience who wanted to learn how to make a perfect omelet. I've made thousands of omelets; it's the test I give my cooks when they apply for a job. This particular omelet didn't work at all. It stuck to the pan, but it was still fine. When we got done with the show, they asked, "Did I want to reshoot it?" I said absolutely not. I want people to see that even with someone who is a professional, these things could happen and there's no reason to get frustrated, it's still delicious. Maybe I wouldn't serve it in my restaurant, but it's fantastic at home.

Q: **You have so many guest stars on the show. Who stands out in your mind as being especially memorable or fun or revealing?**

Michael: The ones that stick out for me are the ones that are actually good cooks. Every star that comes on the show *says* they can cook. You quickly see which ones can or can't. Hugh Jackman came and was very comfortable in the kitchen. He was comfortable in the process. Elisabeth Hasselbeck was very comfortable cooking. Gwyneth Paltrow—super comfortable. You could tell this woman spends a lot of time in the kitchen and has no problem cooking.

WATERMELON GAZPACHO

SERVES 4 | Skill Level: EASY | Prep Time: 15 mins. | Cost: $

I think if Dr. Seuss had ever written a cookbook, he might have come up with the word gazpacho *if it didn't exist already. It's fun to say. Classic gazpacho combines the freshest, ripest summer vegetables in a cooling, thirst-quenching recipe. When I think of summer, I also picture juicy, sweet watermelon, so the thought occurred to me: Why not make my own gazpacho with watermelon? Add some yogurt or sour cream, and it becomes silky smooth. If you want an extra little kick for a summer brunch, skip the Bloody Marys and add some tequila to this recipe.*

6 ripe tomatoes, chopped

2 cups fresh watermelon, chopped, plus more to garnish

2 medium seedless or English cucumbers, peeled and chopped

¾ cup sweet onion, chopped

½ jalapeño pepper, minced (optional)

1 clove garlic, minced

¼ cup flat-leaf parsley, chopped

¼ cup fresh mint, chopped

¼ cup red wine vinegar

¼ cup lime juice

1 cup tomato juice, for consistency

¼ cup feta cheese, crumbled, to garnish

Tabasco, to serve

Worcestershire, to serve

1. Process all the ingredients in a food processor or blender until smooth. Refrigerate until cold, but overnight is better. Pour into a serving bowl and garnish with the crumbled feta and some chopped watermelon. Serve with Tabasco sauce and Worcestershire sauce on the side.

WHITE GAZPACHO WITH FROZEN GRAPES

SERVES 4 | **Skill Level: EASY** | **Cook Time: 10 mins.** | **Prep Time: 10 mins.** | **Cost: $**

This is inspired by the Spanish favorite known as sopa de ajo, *which translates as garlic soup. I didn't think that would sound so appealing in English, so I changed it to White Gazpacho. It reminds me of the way one of the legends of the New York restaurant world, Sirio Maccioni, decided to serve cured lard in his very fancy place. He called it white prosciutto, and it became a favorite of the forerunners of the* Sex *and the City* girls, Manhattan's "ladies who lunch." *Frozen grapes make for a surprising and flavorful treat in your soupspoon.*

1 cup whole almonds, blanched

2 cloves garlic, minced

½ cup sherry vinegar

4 ice cubes

1 cup extra virgin olive oil

Sea salt

1 bunch seedless grapes, halved and frozen

Grated zest of 2 lemons

1. Put the almonds in a small saucepan, cover with cold water, and bring to a boil. Turn off the heat and let stand for 10 minutes, to soften slightly.

2. Drain the almonds, transfer to a blender, and add the garlic, vinegar, and 4 cups cold water. Blend until smooth, about 1 minute. With the motor running, add the ice cubes, then add the olive oil in a slow, steady stream, blending until thoroughly combined. Season with salt, and refrigerate until chilled.

3. Divide the grapes and zest between four small bowls, pour the soup over, and serve.

GRILLED VEGETABLE AND PEACH SUMMER SALAD

SERVES 4 | Skill Level: **EASY** | Cook Time: 15 mins. | Prep Time: 15 mins. | Cost: $

I grew up in New Jersey. They don't call it the Garden State for nothing. It has the most delicious vegetables: sweet corn, beautiful tomatoes, endless zucchini. And in August, when the peaches ripen, I'm in heaven. This recipe was born out of my love for these hallmarks of summer in New Jersey. Or maybe I should say reborn, because it started with some leftover vegetables that we had made the night before. Then some grilled peaches and a fresh dressing. It's the whole flavor profile of summer. Serve it with grilled chicken or sliced steak, and it's a perfect summer supper.

FOR THE SALAD:

2 ears sweet corn

2 medium zucchini, sliced lengthwise

1 bunch asparagus, tough ends removed

2 yellow peaches, pitted and cut into quarters

2 heads romaine, finely chopped

3 Persian cucumbers, sliced into thin rounds

2 avocados, diced

2 cups cherry tomatoes, halved

12 leaves fresh basil, shredded

FOR THE DRESSING:

8 tablespoons extra virgin olive oil

4 tablespoons red wine vinegar

2 tablespoons shallots, minced

2 teaspoons Dijon mustard

2 teaspoons honey or maple syrup

1 tablespoon fresh lemon juice, plus lemon wedges for garnish

½ teaspoon fresh ground coriander

Salt, to taste

Pepper, to taste

1. Shuck the corn and grill on a hot grill or cast-iron griddle until kernels are golden brown and some have slightly charred, rotating to cook all kernels evenly. Remove from the grill to cool. Once cool, remove the corn from the cob and set aside. Grill the zucchini and asparagus until tender, about 2–3 minutes. Grill the peaches flesh side down just until heated through, about 1 minute. Remove the vegetables and peaches from the grill and chop. Add the grilled vegetables and peaches to a large bowl, and add the rest of the salad ingredients. Blend all the dressing ingredients until emulsified in a blender. Toss the salad with the vinaigrette and serve with fresh lemon wedges.

SWEET CORN WITH ONIONS AND BASIL

SERVES 10 | Skill Level: EASY | Cook Time: 50 mins. | Prep Time: 15 mins. | Cost: $

Sweet corn, sweet basil, and sweet Vidalia onions—that's my idea of a sweet and savory summer dish. It's not much more difficult to make than corn on the cob, and when these vegetables are at their peak it is a divine combination. As for jalapeños . . . why not? Corn and hot peppers are two of the great gifts of the Americas to the world. They make great dance partners.

2 Vidalia onions, sliced into ½-inch slices

¼ cup extra virgin olive oil

Salt, to taste

10 ears fresh corn, shucked

1 cup basil leaves

4 Fresno or jalapeño peppers, seeded and thinly sliced

Juice and zest of 2 lemons

1½ teaspoons sugar (optional)

Pepper, to taste

1. Preheat the oven to 400 °F.

2. Toss the onions in 3 tablespoons olive oil, and season with salt. Spread out on a large baking dish and roast until tender, about 20 minutes. Transfer to a large bowl and set aside.

3. Place the corn on the same baking sheet and drizzle with the remaining olive oil and roast, tossing every few minutes, for 15 minutes. Add to the bowl with the onion, along with the remaining ingredients, and toss to combine. Serve warm or at room temperature.

SUMMER SCAFATA

SERVES 6 | **Skill Level: EASY** | **Cook Time: 20–25 mins.** | **Prep Time: 20 mins.** | **Cost: $**

The French, with their ratatouille, may think they've cornered the market on fun words for a vegetable stew, but all that means is they have never heard of the dish called scafata. It's a traditional Friulian dish that the great Lidia Bastianich first made for me. Ah, Lidia! She is such a gentle critic. She will say ten nice things about you before she mentions that you burned the chicken to a crisp! Her scafata is a stew of spring vegetables. I liked it so well, I figured I'd try it with summer vegetables, and the following recipe was my reward.

¼ cup extra virgin olive oil

½ Spanish onion, thinly sliced

1 teaspoon hot red chili flakes

1 large bulb fennel, diced

2 pounds zucchini, cut into ½-inch-thick chunks

2 pounds ripe tomatoes, cut into chunks

1 tablespoon freshly ground black pepper

Kosher salt

¼ cup basil leaves

Drizzle of good balsamic, optional

1. Heat the olive oil in a 12-inch sauté pan or Dutch oven. Add the onion, red pepper flakes, and fennel, and cook until the fennel is tender, about 8 minutes. Add the zucchini, tomatoes, and pepper, and cook over medium-low heat until the zucchini and tomatoes have broken down a bit, about 10–15 minutes. Season with salt.

2. Tear the basil leaves into pieces, sprinkle over the scafata, and serve. This dish is also good at room temperature, or served over grilled or toasted bread with a drizzle of good balsamic.

GRILLED EGGPLANT WITH GREEK YOGURT

SERVES 6 TO 8 | Skill Level: EASY | Cook Time: 12–15 mins. | Prep Time: 15 mins. | Cost: $

Once again, my Mediterranean background—specifically Turkish—comes into play. Eggplant was one of the most common ingredients in our family's cooking when I grew up, but it's often a vegetable that many Americans are afraid of cooking. I think that's because we don't know how to make it except for eggplant parm, or frying it in buckets of oil. Nothing could be easier than this recipe. You wash the eggplant, grill it, and top it with a savory and creamy yogurt sauce, and you're good to go.

4 Japanese eggplants

¼ cup plus 1½ tablespoons extra virgin olive oil

Salt, to taste

Pepper, to taste

2 teaspoons fresh thyme (leaves only)

2 teaspoons fresh oregano (leaves only)

1 cup Greek yogurt

2 cloves garlic, minced

1 teaspoon cayenne pepper

1 tablespoon honey, plus more for garnish

1 tablespoon red wine vinegar

2 tablespoons mint leaves, finely chopped, for garnish

1 cup walnuts, roughly chopped, for garnish

1. Cut the eggplants in half lengthwise, and score the flesh without piercing the skin in a crisscross pattern. Toss the eggplant with ¼ cup of the olive oil, salt, pepper, and the thyme and oregano leaves. Set aside to marinate for up to 20 minutes.

2. Preheat the grill or grill pan to medium-high heat.

3. Place the eggplant on a hot part of the grill and cook until slightly charred, about 3 minutes per side. Transfer to a cooler part of the grill or grill pan, and cook through, until soft when pierced with a knife, about 8 more minutes. Remove to a platter and set aside.

4. Meanwhile, make the sauce by whisking together the yogurt, minced garlic, remaining olive oil, cayenne pepper, honey, and red wine vinegar. Season with salt and pepper.

5. To serve, top the eggplant with a generous portion of sauce and garnish with mint, chopped walnuts, and another drizzle of honey.

Eggplants are easy . . . really!

Eggplant plus heat source pretty much tells the story. Basically, you roast an eggplant the way you would roast a pepper, turning it as each side shrivels and chars. The skin will shrink as the water pushes out, leaving you with a sad-looking, shriveled eggplant. Don't worry, that's how you want it, because when you cut it in half the insides are creamy soft and easy to scoop out.

DAPHNE'S SUPERFOODS SMOOTHIE

SERVES 1 | **Skill Level: EASY** | **Prep Time: 5 mins.** | **Cost: $**

When I was little, my parents had their hands full trying to get me to eat a healthy breakfast. I guess that means I was a pretty normal child. The world knows my dad as the super health expert Dr. Oz, but to me he's just Daddy, and when your daddy is a nutrition expert, he will do whatever he can to make sure his daughter eats right. His solution was a delicious smoothie, chock-full of fresh fruit and yogurt. He called it the "Magic Drink." Now that I am no longer a little girl, I have learned to add some more good-for-you ingredients to my magic drink. The Chew gang had a lot of fun teasing me when I told them my superfoods smoothie gets a boost from psyllium husks. Psyllium is just extra fiber. This is a good thing. Fiber leaves you satisfyingly full and aids in good digestion. I have yet to meet somebody who has tried this smoothie who doesn't like it.

½ cup yogurt (plain or flavored, but avoid artificial sweeteners)

1 cup fresh fruit of your choosing

1 teaspoon honey (optional)

½ banana (optional)

1 tablespoon psyllium husks

3 500-milligram ester-c capsules (about 1 tablespoon)

1 cup ice (or frozen fruit and skip ice)

Water, to blend for consistency

Juice, to blend for consistency

1. Combine the ingredients in a blender and blend until smooth and creamy. If you have trouble blending, try adding a little water or juice to thin the smoothie. Make sure to have at least two 8-ounce glasses of water with each serving of smoothie to help the psyllium husks expand so they digest properly.

Daphne gets a surprise visit from her dad, Dr. Oz.

MUSSELS ALLA PIASTRA

SERVES 6 | **Skill Level: EASY** | **Cook Time: 15 mins.** | **Prep time: 10 mins.** | **Cost: $$**

If you are ever on the coast of Emilia-Romagna, south of Venice and north of Ancona, chances are you will eat some seafood made on a griddle—that's piastra *in Italian. And when you return to the States, chances are even greater you are going to want to eat more seafood made this way. It's actually quite simple: some seafood, some lemon, some bread crumbs, and that about tells the tale. Don't let me forget prosciutto! In Emilia-Romagna, even if you order a vegetarian dish, they're probably going to sneak some prosciutto in there. They don't think of it as meat. It's a seasoning. I agree. There's very little in cooking that can't be improved with a little prosciutto.*

3 dozen small mussels, scrubbed and debearded

Extra virgin olive oil

Salt

Pepper

1 cup bread crumbs

4 tablespoons prosciutto, coarsely chopped

1 bunch lemon thyme (leaves only)

Grated zest and juice of 1 orange

Grated zest and juice of 1 lemon

1 jalapeño, thinly sliced

½ bunch chives, thinly sliced

2 tablespoons white wine

1. Preheat a griddle or piastra over medium-high heat.

2. Put the mussels in a large metal bowl. Drizzle with some olive oil and season with salt and pepper.

3. Place the bread crumbs, prosciutto, lemon thyme, orange and lemon zest and juice, jalapeño, and chives in a food processor, and pulse until well mixed, 6 or 7 pulses.

4. Add the bread crumb mixture to the mussels, and toss to combine.

5. Pour 2 tablespoons olive oil onto the griddle. Working quickly, dump the mussels (with everything else in the bowl) onto the griddle. Add a splash of white wine, and cover with the inverted bowl. You may have to cook the mussels in batches if your griddle isn't large enough. Remove the bowl after 2 minutes, and gently stir the mussels around. Continue cooking, uncovered, for about 3 minutes longer, until they all open (discard any that do not open); transfer the mussels to a platter. Scrape up any bread crumb mixture remaining on the griddle, and scatter it over the mussels. Squeeze a little extra lemon juice on top and serve immediately.

The iron age

In Italy, they call it a *piastra*. In Spain, it's a *plancha*. In America, it's a cast-iron griddle. For most of us, we use it to make pancakes and that's about it, but it's really a wonderful tool for making fish, steaks, chops, vegetables, flatbreads, and even desserts outside on a grill. If even heat is what you are looking for, think *grrr . . .* as in *Griddles Are Great!*

FRIED CLAM SANDWICH

SERVES 4 | **Skill Level: EASY** | **Cook Time: 4 mins.** | **Prep Time: 15 mins.** | **Cost: $**

My wife, Lizzie, lived in Boston before we met, and, on a later visit there, she took me for my first really great fried clams. We ate our way through piles of clam sandwiches, steamed lobsters, the whole thing. I wondered: How did they get such perfection? Try as I might, I couldn't figure it out. Instead of overthinking it, which we chefs sometimes to, I went in the kitchen and asked them how they did it. Some chefs treat these things as The Secret of the Ages. Not these guys. They told me right off the bat: evaporated milk and corn flour, and fry them in lard, that's it. Moral of the story: quite often the greatest things in life are the simplest.

Canola oil, for frying

¼ cup all-purpose flour

Salt

Pepper

1 egg, lightly beaten

1 12-ounce can evaporated milk

½ cup panko bread crumbs

2 dozen Littleneck clams, shucked

¼ cup tartar sauce (recipe follows)

4 potato hot dog buns

Lemon wedges, for garnish

1. Preheat the oil to 375 °F.

2. Create a dredging station by placing three baking dishes side by side. The first dish will be the flour, seasoned generously with salt and pepper. The second dish will be the egg and evaporated milk, beaten together. The third baking dish will be the panko bread crumbs.

3. Dredge the clams first into the flour, then the egg mixture, then the panko, and drop them into the hot oil. Fry until golden brown, about 3–4 minutes.

4. Spread a generous amount of tartar sauce on each of the buns, and divide the clams evenly among the four buns. Serve with lemon wedges.

TARTAR SAUCE

1 cup mayonnaise

½ cup sour cream

2 tablespoons capers

2 tablespoons pickles

1 tablespoon parsley, chopped

1 tablespoon horseradish

Juice of ½ a lemon

Salt, to taste

Pepper, to taste

1. Mix all ingredients until combined. Refrigerate until ready to serve.

Michael I like fried chicken so much that when I make it I fry it twice. Once to cook it, seal in flavor, and begin to crisp it, and then a second time to add even more flavor and crunchiness. As far as I am concerned, you can't get too much crispness or too much flavor. I like to mix my seasonings and then coat the chicken parts with it and leave them overnight. All of that flavor mingles and mixes and creeps up into the chicken. Then, the next day I dredge the chicken pieces in flour, and for the moment of truth—actually, about 22 minutes of truth—I fry the chicken. What kind of oil do I use, you ask? No kind of oil. I'm a good old-fashioned lard guy.

So first I fry it in hot oil with some garlic for extra nutty flavor, and then I finish with a second frying with rosemary and sage for even more extra flavor.

MICHAEL SYMON'S TWICE-FRIED CHICKEN

SERVES 6 | Skill Level: EASY | Cook Time: 30 mins. | Prep Time: 15 mins. | COST: $$

2 tablespoons seafood seasoning

1 tablespoon coriander seeds, toasted and cracked

1 teaspoon chipotle powder

1 teaspoon smoked paprika

Kosher salt

1 4- to 5-pound chicken, cut into 12 pieces

1½ cups instant flour (such as Wondra)

3 tablespoons honey (optional), plus more for garnish

Sriracha (optional)

Vegetable oil or lard, for frying

6 cloves garlic, skin on

2 strips bacon

4 sprigs rosemary

4 leaves sage

Freshly grated Parmesan, for garnish

1. In a small bowl, combine the seafood seasoning, coriander seeds, chipotle powder, paprika, and a generous pinch of salt, and mix well. Coat the chicken pieces with the spice mixture, and place in a bag to refrigerate overnight.

2. If you decide to make this a spicy dish, in a small bowl, combine the honey and Sriracha. Stir well and refrigerate until ready to fry the chicken.

3. Remove the chicken pieces from the refrigerator and dredge in flour.

4. In a large Dutch oven, put in enough lard to come 4 inches up the side of the pot. Heat the lard to 300–325 °F.

5. Add garlic and bacon to the hot oil and fry for a couple of minutes.

6. Beginning with the thighs, add the chicken to the pot, making sure not to crowd. (This may take several batches.) Cook until golden and cooked 80 percent through, 8–10 minutes. Remove the chicken to a wire cooling rack, and repeat with the remaining chicken, if necessary.

7. Once all the chicken is done, raise the heat of the lard to 365 °F. Add rosemary and sage to fry and season the oil, fry 2–3 minutes then remove to a paper towel. Add the chicken in the same batches, and cook until dark golden and crispy, 2–3 minutes. Remove onto paper towels and serve immediately, topped with a drizzle of honey, a pinch of salt, and some freshly grated Parmesan.

Bacon's good too

Sometimes it's hard to find lard in the market. Or maybe you prefer to cook with oil. Either way, for yet another flavor booster, I toss a couple of slices of bacon in the hot oil. Daphne says basically my method is to cook fat in fat. I say, anything that adds flavor can't be bad.

GRANDMA THELMA'S FRIED CHICKEN

SERVES 6 | Skill Level: EASY | Cook Time: 8–10 mins. | Prep Time: 10 mins. | Cost: $

Inactive Prep Time: 12 hrs.

FOR THE DRY RUB:

1 tablespoon salt

1 tablespoon black pepper

1 tablespoon garlic powder

1 tablespoon onion powder

1 tablespoon cayenne pepper

1 small organic chicken, broken down into 10 pieces

Peanut oil, for frying

FOR THE BATTER:

3 eggs

1 cup buttermilk

¼ cup water

2–3 cups flour, to dredge

2 tablespoons cornstarch

Salt

Pepper

1. In a mixing bowl, combine the salt, pepper, garlic powder, onion powder, and cayenne pepper. Combine the spice mixture and chicken pieces in a plastic zip bag, and toss to coat. Refrigerate overnight.

2. Preheat ½ inch of peanut oil in a cast-iron skillet to 360 °F.

3. Lightly beat the eggs, and combine with the buttermilk and water in a shallow dish. In another shallow dish, add the flour and cornstarch, and then season with salt and pepper. Dip each chicken piece into the buttermilk mixture and then coat in flour mixture. Fry the pieces until golden brown on all sides, about 3–4 minutes per side.

4. Remove to a wire rack to drain excess oil, then serve.

Carla My fried chicken isn't really *my* fried chicken. Like a lot of good things in my cooking, it comes from my Grandma Thelma. She wasn't on *Top Chef* like me, but if *Top Chef* had the guts to have some grandmas on, Thelma would've knocked Tom Colicchio's socks off. Like Michael, I season my chicken the night before to give the flavors a chance to make their presence known. Next day, I dip the chicken parts in an egg-buttermilk batter and then dredge in some flour. It adds up to one heck of a crispy crust. Michael may need to fry his twice, but Grandma Thelma's is such a flavor powerhouse that once is plenty—make that plenty good!

FETTUCCINE WITH LOBSTER, TOMATOES, AND SAFFRON

SERVES 6 | Skill Level: **EASY** | Cook Time: **20–25 mins.** | Prep Time: **20 mins.** | Cost: **$-$$-$$$**

Three recipes in one: first I do it simple, then I throw in another ingredient that makes it special, then I add still another and it's spectacular. Actually, with the right ingredients and a good cook, they're all spectacular. So first we have pasta with onion, celery, garlic, and potatoes. Real simple and real good.

Then I add in a little saffron, which ups the price about a buck a serving but gives the dish a special something.

Then I dice up some lobster meat, which adds a good ten to twelve dollars, but, hey, it's still a darn sight cheaper than lobster in a restaurant. Make sure you chop your lobster into bite-sized pieces so that you can use your fork to pick up both pasta and a lobster chunk for a bite-sized mouthful.

Salt

4 2½-pound lobsters, steamed 10 minutes and cooled

4 tablespoons extra virgin olive oil

1 medium red onion, cut into ⅛-inch julienne

2 stalks celery, cut into ¼-inch dice

2 medium waxy potatoes, cut into ⅛-inch dice

4 cloves garlic, thinly sliced

½ pound overripe tomatoes, cut into ½-inch dice with juices, or 1 can whole peeled San Marzano

¼ cup dry white wine

Pinch of saffron

1½ pounds fettuccine

½ cup chopped fresh chives

1. Bring 8 quarts water to a boil in a large spaghetti pot and add 2 tablespoons salt.

2. Remove the lobster meat from the shells and cut into ¼-inch pieces.

3. In a 14-inch sauté pan, heat the olive oil until smoking. Add the onion, celery, potatoes, and garlic, and sauté until golden brown, 6–7 minutes.

4. Add the tomatoes, wine, and saffron, and bring to a boil. Lower the heat and simmer for 3 minutes.

5. Drop the fettuccine into the boiling water and cook to 1 minute less than the package instructions. Just before it is done, carefully ladle ½ cup of the fettuccine water into the pan with the sauce.

6. Add the lobster to the tomato sauce in the pan and toss through. Drain the pasta in a colander and dump into the pan with the sauce, add the chives, and toss over medium heat, about 30 seconds, until nicely coated.

7. Pour into a bowl and serve.

Tomato tip

In season, you can't beat fresh tomatoes, but during the rest of the year, you'll do much better with a great canned tomato, like the ones they harvest in San Marzano.

SUMMER

187

CORN DOGGIN'

SERVES 6 | Skill Level: EASY | Cook Time: 10 mins. | Prep Time: 15 mins. | Cost: $$

If you grew up in the Midwest, you know what I am talking about when I mention corn dogs: hot dogs fried in a sweet and savory corn batter and topped with whatever struck your fancy, and since those were the days before fancy food, that meant mustard, mayo, or ketchup. I made my rep in the 1990s taking comfort food like this and upscaling it a little bit. Those were great days. All I did was work, party, and sleep. To tell you the truth, it was so much fun I don't remember a lot of it. One day I said to myself, "What if I corn dogged some lobster, shrimp, sausage, or zucchini?" I did, and they all were great. So were all the endless toppings and dips you can come up with.

Vegetable oil, for frying

12 colossal shrimp, shelled and deveined with tails only, or hot dogs, or zucchini spears

FOR THE BATTER:

1 cup flour

1 cup corn meal

2 tablespoons sugar

1 egg, lightly beaten

½ teaspoon baking powder

1 cup milk

Kosher salt

FOR THE CHIPOTLE MAYO:

1 cup mayonnaise

Juice and zest of ½ lime

3 tablespoons pureed chipotle in adobo

2 tablespoons chives, finely chopped

SPECIAL EQUIPMENT:

Skewers

TO MAKE THE CORN DOG:

1. Preheat the oil to 365 °F.

2. Thread a skewer through each of the shrimp, from head to tail.

3. In a shallow baking dish, mix together the batter ingredients until a smooth batter is formed. Batter each of the shrimp.

4. Fry each of the shrimp in the oil until crispy and golden brown, about 2 minutes. Do this in batches, if necessary. Transfer to drain on a paper towel–lined plate.

TO MAKE THE CHIPOTLE MAYO:

5. In a small bowl, whisk together the mayonnaise, lime juice, and chipotle until it is consistently incorporated. Fold in the chives.

6. Serve the chipotle mayo alongside the shrimp.

Better batter

You can buy store-bought batter mix, but it often has a ton of sugar. As with most things in cooking, you are always better off making your own from scratch. As Carla pointed out to me when I started lecturing on the fine points of batter making to fill time on the show, "Hey, it's cornbread with more milk in it." Leave it to Carla to bring it back to basics.

BIG MIKE BURGER

SERVES 4 | **Skill Level: EASY** | **Cook Time: 10 mins.** | **Prep Time: 20 mins.** | **Cost: $**

We all know the Big Mac. This is the Big Mike. I know I'm tootin' my own horn a little, but my burgers have taken the top prize at the South Beach Wine and Food Festival three years in a row, so I hope that gives me the right to a few extra words on America's—and maybe the world's—favorite food, the burger.

You could make this with regular supermarket burger meat, but I find a custom mix, made from scratch, is what separates great burgers from regular old burgers. My preferred mix is about 75 percent meat and 25 percent fat.

There are two kinds of burgers. One I call the diner burger and the other is the bar burger. A diner burger is thin. When you grill it, you get a crunchy, crusty, salty texture on the outside and the meat is medium to medium-well all the way through. A bar burger is thicker and takes longer to cook and develop a crust, but you can pick the amount of doneness. The Big Mike is a double-patty diner burger.

These burgers are designed for a griddle. Griddling is the best way I know to get all those beautiful crunchies. Don't forget you can always put a griddle outside on the barbecue.

Then you've got your sauce. Get inventive. This one has a garlic aioli—a kind of tangy mayonnaise—with some hot sauce and, to finish it off, my secret ingredient: a little pickle juice.

And you must toast the bun. Serving a burger on an untoasted bun is a sin. You put it all together—maybe with some pickles, lettuce, tomatoes, and on-ions—smoosh it down a bit, and take a nice big bite. Don't worry if you get some juice running down your arm. That's Nature's way of telling you that you made a great burger.

Melted cheese is a must

If you are going to put cheese on your burger, then make sure it's melted. There's a neat trick to this. Lay a slice of cheese on the patty, then spritz a little water on the griddle next to the burger and immediately cover the burger with anything dome-shaped that won't melt on the griddle. The super-hot steam melts the cheese and saturates the burger with juiciness.

SUMMER

189

2 pounds ground beef
(75-25 blend)

Salt

Pepper

4 slices aged Cheddar cheese

2 tablespoons butter

4 brioche rolls, cut into
thirds, like a Big Mac

FOR THE SPECIAL SAUCE:

¼ cup garlic aioli

¼ cup brown mustard

¼ cup ketchup

Hot sauce, to taste

Pickle juice, to taste

Sweet Hot Pickles and
Peppers, to serve

Pickled red onions, to serve
(recipe follows)

1 cup romaine lettuce,
shredded, to serve

1. Preheat a griddle over medium heat.

2. Make eight equal-sized patties from the ground beef, about ½ inch bigger than the bun you want to serve it on. Season with salt and pepper.

3. Cook the patties on the griddle, about 3 minutes per side. Top four of the patties with slices of cheese when cooking the second side. Set aside.

4. Butter the brioche and toast on the griddle until golden brown.

5. Make the special sauce by whisking together the garlic aioli, mustard, and ketchup. Add a couple dashes of hot sauce and a splash of pickle juice.

6. Assemble with the cheesed patty on the bottom, topped with pickles and onions. Add the middle bun, then the second patty. Top with special sauce, shredded romaine, and the top bun.

PICKLED RED ONIONS

2 pounds red onions, sliced

3–3 ½ cups white wine
vinegar

2 tablespoons sugar

2 tablespoons kosher salt

2 teaspoons mustard seeds

1 tablespoon crushed red
pepper flakes

2 tablespoons coriander
seeds

2 tablespoons black
peppercorns

4 garlic cloves

2 bay leaves

1. Pack the onions into two 1-quart jars and cover with water to come within ½ inch of the rim. Pour the water out into a measuring cup. Note the volume, pour off half the water, and replace with vinegar. Add 2 tablespoons sugar and 2 tablespoons salt for every 3 cups of liquid.

2. Pour the vinegar mixture into a nonreactive saucepan, add the mustard seeds, red pepper flakes, coriander seeds, black peppercorns, garlic, and bay leaves, and bring to a boil over high heat. Allow the liquid to boil for 2 minutes, and then remove it from the heat.

3. Pour hot liquid into the jars to cover the onions and screw on the lids. Refrigerate for up to 1 month.

Food, Fire, and Family: Memories of the Grill

Michael

My dad felt he was the master of fire, and we let him think that because he was pretty good, but the truth is everybody worked the grill, including my mom. We did lots of lamb and a ton of spit roasting. A couple of times throughout the year, we made lamb or goat on a spit just brushed with olive oil and oregano and a little bit of red wine and vinegar. We always used hardwood charcoal. It makes the best heat and has the best flavor. My favorite grill meal these days: rib-eye with tomato salad. Perfection!!

Mario

In my family, everything went on the fire. The division of labor was pretty old-fashioned: the boys got the fire and the ladies got the kitchen, but everyone cooked— grandmas, grandpas, uncles, aunts, cousins.

All of my cousins, particularly on my mom's side, were big fishermen: they owned, like, half the state records for steelhead and salmon. There were also lots of hunters in the family, so after every fishing or hunting trip, they would bring back their edible trophies and grill them, smoke them, cure them, hang them.

We always did hot smoked salmon and planked salmon on cedar. That burned flavor was so delicious and unforgettable. Not only salmon. We grilled, smoked, and roasted duck every way you could dream of.

We had a spit roaster, and we did everything from chickens to legs of lamb all over open wood fire or lump charcoal. We even had the Green Egg back in its prototype days in the late 1970s. For us, the idea of using fire for food was one of the basics of life.

Carla

My go-to barbecue meal is pulled pork shoulder like they used to make at Mary's down on Jefferson Street, in Nashville, Tennessee. It was the greatest. Of course, people in the other part of town, East Nashville, had their own favorite, and they would swear by it just as religiously. All over town, you'd see those big oil drums that they'd use to smoke pork, and every smoker had its true believers. Bottom line, I want pulled pork on a soft bun with pickles and coleslaw.

And then it's all about the sides too. You have to have potato salad. Also grilled corn. I like corn, but I *love* grilled corn, especially with butter and something tangy like lemon and lime. Delish! And you absolutely need some coleslaw. I used to want it very mayonnaise-y, but just like with the grilled corn, I now look for a good bit of tang, so I pickle my cabbage in vinegar and then add a little mayonnaise.

The great thing about a barbecue is you can feed so many people. I like to keep mine to twenty, but somehow they often end up being thirty or forty and somehow there's always enough.

Clinton

I grew up on Long Island, and we grilled as much as possible. My dad would be in the backyard grilling in the middle of winter, if possible. In my adult life, it's very rare that I cook indoors on a hot day in the middle of the summer, so I'm a big fan of chicken thighs on the grill. It's one of those things that you can be three sheets to the wind and still destroy on the grill. This isn't a recommendation for grilling while incredibly intoxicated, but you can talk and grill chicken thighs and not feel like you have to be spending all your time staring at them,

wondering if they're done or not. I'm big on steaks too. For sides, I love grilled asparagus—that's my favorite. I need to get Mario to show me how to plank a salmon. I so want to do that.

Daphne

One of my favorite memories was going to visit my grandparents and having my grandpa throw a whole fish on the grill. It was the simplest preparation: fresh-caught fish, a little bit of fresh olive oil and lemon. I don't know why more people don't try it. A whole fish is hard to mess up and sooo delicious.

Grilling is one of the best ways to bring a family together, because everyone can do something. I'm one of four children. My mom was one of six. So when our family gets together for a barbecue, it can be a lot of people—like thirty-five! Grilling is the easiest way I know to feed a big group. My fave specialty is grilled corn, Mexican-style. I think Carla would second that emotion.

Amani Toomer officiates a grill-off in the rain.

193

CHEESE-STUFFED MORTADELLA ON BRUSCHETTA

SERVES 6–8 | **Skill Level: EASY** | **Cook Time: 6–8 mins.** | **Prep Time: 20 mins.** | **Cost: $**

Great Italian appetizers are less about technique and more about buying the right stuff. That's actually true of all cuisine. Mortadella, also called baloney because it comes from Bologna, is a wonderful cold cut, so smooth as it slides over your tongue when you have it sliced super thin. Sometimes it has pistachios in it. Robiola cheese is, to my way of thinking, the sexiest cream cheese of all time. It's from Piemonte. When he saw me putting this together, Michael couldn't resist chiming in with, "I love this, Batali is making baloney and cream cheese sandwiches." He had a point; you could use regular old baloney instead of mortadella, and cream cheese works too. You roll 'em up with a basil leaf, cook 'em up on a grill pan. Finito!

12–14 thin slices mortadella, without pistachios

12–14 ounces fresh Robiola

12–14 fresh basil leaves

Olive oil

½ baguette, sliced

3 cups baby arugula

1 tablespoon red wine vinegar

Coarse sea salt

Black pepper

SPECIAL EQUIPMENT:

Toothpicks

1. Preheat a gas grill or prepare a fire in a charcoal grill.

2. Lay the mortadella out on a work surface. Place 2 tablespoons of the cheese in the very center of each slice. Place a basil leaf on top of each mound of cheese. Fold the bottom of each slice over the cheese, then fold over the sides and roll the cheese up in the mortadella. Secure each with a toothpick.

3. Place the mortadella packets seam side up on the hottest part of the grill and cook until lightly charred on the bottom, about 2 minutes. Turn over and repeat on the second side, about 2 minutes longer. Transfer to a platter, and remove the toothpicks from each packet.

4. Brush the slices of bread with a little olive oil and grill, about 30 seconds per side. Place a mortadella packet on each piece of bread.

5. In a medium bowl, toss the arugula with 3 tablespoons olive oil and then the vinegar. Season with coarse sea salt and black pepper, and pile the greens over the hot and delightful mortadella packets.

TURKEY SLIDERS

SERVES 4 | **Skill Level: EASY** | **Cook Time: 8–10 mins.** | **Prep Time: 20 mins.** | **Cost: $**

I basically live on these in the summer, and people say that I make the world's best turkey sliders. People aren't just saying that to be nice. You can always tell the sincere complimenters from the people pretending they like something by who goes back for seconds . . . and thirds. When we made this on The Chew, *I seasoned it, but Mario walked over and picked up the pepper grinder to give it another two million turns. That's the difference between a restaurant chef and a home cook. The resto guys ain't shy about seasoning.*

1 pound ground turkey

1 onion, grated

2 tablespoons Dijon mustard

1 egg

½ cup panko bread crumbs

1 teaspoon cumin

Salt, to taste

Pepper, to taste

1 package of 8 mini potato buns

FOR THE TOPPINGS:

Ketchup

Dijon mustard

Mayonnaise

Tomato

Lettuce

1. Preheat a grill pan over medium-high heat. In a large bowl, mix the turkey, grated onion, Dijon mustard, egg, panko, cumin, salt, and pepper until combined. Mold the mixture into small patties. Grill the patties for 3–4 minutes per side or until cooked completely through. Remove from grill, and build the sliders on potato buns.

Shapely is good

When I have combined all the main ingredients, if it's too mushy, I add Japanese panko bread crumbs (they really hold their crunch) until the patty will stay together.

Done plus one

Turkey must be cooked all the way through. When you think that they're done, cook them another minute. I have never overcooked a burger using this method.

Always add a whole grated
onion to the recipe. Because
turkey has to cook all the
way through, it can dry out.
Onions add moistness and
sweet flavor.

197

DAPHNE'S BEST BURGER

SERVES 4 | **Skill Level: EASY** | **Cook Time: 25 mins.** | **Prep Time: 20 mins.** | **Cost: $**

Calling all meat eaters! This tempura mushroom burger is guaranteed to make the most committed carnivore swoon. There are tons of veggie burgers out there—cashew curry burgers, grain-based burgers, tofu burgers—but if I had to pick one, this gets my vote. The secret is portabella mushroom and crunchy tempura. When you put it in a burger with all the toppings and condiments, it nearly fools your palate into thinking that it's meat. Deep-thinking chefs say that's because it has that mysterious flavor called umami. *If you're not familiar with* umami, *it's the Japanese word for "yummy." Finally, topping with a roasted garlic and tarragon aioli puts my burger's flavor off the charts.*

8 portabella mushroom caps, plus 2 cups portabella stems, minced

1 tablespoon olive oil

2 shallots, minced

FOR THE TEMPURA BATTER:

1 cup all-purpose flour

2 tablespoons cornstarch

½ teaspoon salt

3 egg whites, stiffly beaten

1 cup seltzer

Vegetable oil, for frying

4 onion brioche buns

Garlic Tarragon Aioli (recipe follows)

SPECIAL EQUIPMENT:

16 toothpicks

FOR THE TOPPINGS:

Lettuce

Tomato

1. Preheat the oven to 350 °F.

2. Place the mushroom caps on a baking sheet and put in the oven for 12–15 minutes, until soft. This helps take moisture out of the mushroom for a better fry. Remove the mushrooms from the oven and pat dry excess moisture.

3. In a medium sauté pan, heat 1 tablespoon olive oil. Add the portabella stems and shallots. Sauté for 2–3 minutes. Cool mixture and set aside.

4. To make the tempura batter, combine the dry ingredients. Fold in the stiff egg whites and then seltzer.

5. Fill each portabella mushroom cap with the mushroom-shallot mixture. Make a sandwich with another cap, and secure with toothpicks. Dip in the tempura batter, and fry in oil at about 360 °F.

6. Place the fried mushroom caps on a toasted onion bun with aioli and eat 'em up!

Batter up

I use seltzer or soda water in my tempura batter. It keeps it from absorbing too much fat, and the bubbles help keep the batter crispy and light.

GARLIC TARRAGON AIOLI

1 head garlic

Salt

Pepper

2 tablespoons olive oil

1 cup mayo

2 tablespoons fresh tarragon, chopped

1. Cut a head of garlic in half along the equator and place on a piece of foil. Season with salt and pepper and drizzle with olive oil, then fold the foil over garlic to form a pouch. Roast until tender, about 15–20 minutes. Remove from the oven and set aside to cool. Remove the pulp of the garlic from the head, and place in a blender or food processor. Add the mayo and the tarragon, and puree until smooth.

Emeril and Carla demonstrate some classic Southern cooking.

Twice-cooked mushrooms

Portabellas give up a ton of water, so you need to roast them before you batter and fry them. Otherwise you will have a soggy tempura burger, and no one ever used the word *soggy* to describe something delicious.

DRY RUB BABY BACK RIBS WITH SCALLOPED POTATOES

SERVES 6 | **Skill Level: EASY** | **Cook Time: 2 hrs.** | **Prep Time: 30 mins.** | **Cost: $**

Whenever we visit my husband's family in Chicago, my mother-in-law makes these ribs for us. Like all rib makers, she has always kept it a secret, but I am happy to tell you she has given me permission to share it with all Chewsters. It starts, as all great ribs do, with a spice rub. Mario offered to rub my ribs, and it was clear that he didn't mean the spareribs. Naughty boy!

My mother-in-law makes her barbecue sauce from scratch, and I recommend you do the same. Once you taste her ribs, you are going to wish you had my mother-in-law, but too late. I already have dibs on her and the husband to prove it.

FOR THE DRY RUB:

2 tablespoons paprika

2 tablespoons cayenne pepper

1 tablespoon freshly ground black pepper

2 tablespoons garlic powder

2 tablespoons onion powder

2 tablespoons kosher salt

1 tablespoon dried oregano

1 tablespoon dried thyme

2½ pounds baby back ribs

FOR THE BARBECUE SAUCE:

5 tablespoons butter

½ yellow onion, chopped

3 cloves garlic, minced

2 cups tomato sauce

½ cup apple cider vinegar

½ cup light brown sugar

3 tablespoons paprika

1 tablespoon chili powder

TO MAKE THE RIBS:

1. In a medium bowl, combine all the dry rub ingredients and mix thoroughly. Rub the ribs all over with the dry rub, and allow to marinate for at least 1 hour.

2. Meanwhile, in a medium saucepan over medium heat, add the butter. Once it has foamed and subsided, add the onion and cook until softened, about 5 minutes. Add the garlic and cook an additional minute. Add the remaining sauce ingredients and stir until thoroughly mixed. Reduce heat and simmer sauce for 2 hours.

3. Preheat the oven to 350 °F. Place the ribs in a baking dish and cover halfway up with the barbecue sauce, then cook in the oven for at least 2 hours, until meat is tender. Serve with extra barbecue sauce on the side and the scalloped potatoes.

It pays to ask questions

In shopping for ribs, look for lots of marbling and a light pink color, and make sure they haven't been frozen. Even if you shop in a supermarket with aisles a half mile long, remember there is a real live butcher in the meat department. He or she will be able to advise you, and most of them enjoy the chance to go beyond the shrink-wrap and talk to an actual human customer.

FOR THE SCALLOPED POTATOES:

3 tablespoons extra virgin olive oil

3 yellow onions, cut into ¼-inch-thick slices

Pinch of kosher salt

Pinch of freshly ground black pepper

¼ teaspoon sugar

6 tablespoons butter, melted

2½ pounds russet potatoes, peeled and cut into ¼-inch slices

¼ cup flour

3 cups milk

¼ cup Parmesan cheese, grated

¼ cup parsley

TO MAKE THE SCALLOPED POTATOES:

4. Preheat the oven to 350 °F. In a pan over medium heat, add the olive oil. Add the onions and season with a pinch of salt and ground pepper, and the sugar. Cook the onions in an even layer until caramelized, about 30 minutes. In a 9-by-13-inch casserole dish, grease lightly with butter, and add a layer of the potatoes. Alternate layers of potatoes and caramelized onions sprinkled with a large pinch of flour and drizzled with butter. Continue until almost full, then add milk to cover. Top with grated cheese. Bake until bubbling and golden brown, about 1½ hours. Top with parsley to serve.

The Chew crew discovers their inner burlesque babe with the Pussycat Dolls.

T-BONE FIORENTINA

SERVES 6 | **Skill Level: EASY** | **Cook Time: 40–45 mins.** | **Prep Time: 15 mins.** | **COST: $$**

We Americans think of ourselves as steak eaters. The Tuscans think of us more as steak nibblers when they compare an American steak to a classic fiorentina. *It's big and it comes from big steers, the giant breed known as* Chianina. *Rubbed with salt and olive oil and rosemary, the meat develops a great charred, salty, crispy crust and the rosemary puts in mind the scent of a pine forest when the wind blows through it. And that, of course, makes me think of opening great wine. Don't ask me why. All I know is there are a lot of things in this world that make me think of opening a delicious red wine. You can make this on the grill or pan roast.*

2 tablespoons rosemary, chopped

1 tablespoon sage, chopped

1 tablespoon thyme, chopped

2 tablespoons kosher salt

2 tablespoons freshly ground pepper

1 3-pound T-bone steak, about 3 inches thick

2 tablespoons extra virgin olive oil

Juice of ½ a lemon

1. Preheat the oven to 350 °F and preheat a grill or grill pan. In a small bowl, combine the rosemary, sage, thyme, salt, and pepper. Rub the steak with 2 tablespoons of the oil, and then rub with the herb mixture. Grill the steak over medium-high heat until lightly charred all over, about 10 minutes, halfway through. Transfer to a small roasting pan and roast for about 30 minutes, or until an instant-read thermometer inserted into the thickest spot registers 120 °F. Let rest for 10 minutes before slicing. Squeeze a little lemon over the top of the steak.

BLUEBERRY HAND PIES

SERVES 10 | Skill Level: EASY | Cook Time: 20 mins. | Prep Time: 45 mins. | Cost: $

Call it a turnover, or maybe a blueberry empanada, or a baked fruit ravioli, or a dessert taco, or anything you want. I call them Blueberry Hand Pies. These are easier to make than a full-on blueberry pie, and the neat thing is each little hand pie is a single serving of pie. No runny fruit filling puddling in your pie dish. And you can eat a whole piece with your hands without getting your fingers messy, at least in theory. On the other hand, you might want to use a fork if you top it with whipped cream or your favorite flavor ice cream. Fran Drescher helped me make these, and she really liked that it is a dessert but not overly sweet. Daphne gave me extra health points because we made the crust with whole grains: that means added fiber even without her magic psyllium husks (sorry, Daph, couldn't resist).

FOR THE DOUGH:

12 tablespoons unsalted butter, cold

1 cup whole wheat flour

1 cup spelt flour

¼ teaspoon salt

¼ teaspoon baking powder

1½ 3-ounce packages cream cheese, cold, cut into fourths

2 tablespoons ice water

1 tablespoon apple cider vinegar

FOR THE FILLING:

¼ cup sugar

Zest and juice of 1 lemon

3 cups fresh or frozen blueberries

3 tablespoons cornstarch

1 teaspoon salt

TO FINISH:

1 egg

1 tablespoon water

Granulated sugar

TO MAKE THE DOUGH:

1. Cut the butter into small ¾-inch cubes. Wrap in plastic and freeze until frozen solid, about 30 minutes.

2. Place the flours, salt, and baking powder in a gallon-sized plastic freezer bag, and freeze for at least 30 minutes. Place the flour mixture in a food processor with the metal blade attachment, and process for a few seconds to fully combine all the ingredients.

3. Add the cream cheese and pulse until it has achieved a coarse meal texture. Add the frozen butter and continue to pulse until the butter is the size of peas. Next, add the water and vinegar. Continue to pulse until the butter is the size of small peas.

4. At this point, the mixture is not going to hold together. Transfer it back to the plastic freezer bag. Fold the ends of the zipper with your fingers, and knead the mixture with the heels of your hands until the dough holds together in one piece and stretches when pulled. Split the dough into two pieces. Wrap them in plastic, flatten them into discs, and then transfer to the refrigerator for at least 45 minutes, though preferably overnight.

TO MAKE THE FILLING:

5. Combine the sugar, zest, blueberries, and salt. Allow the mixture to sit for 30 minutes, and then strain any excess liquid. Mix in the cornstarch and set aside.

TO MAKE THE PIES:

6. Combine the egg and water in a small bowl.

7. Roll out the dough on a lightly floured work surface to ¼ inch thick. Using the largest ring mold, cut out discs. Spoon 1½ tablespoons of the blueberry filling onto the circle, fold over, and pinch close. Cut a small slit on the hand pie, and brush lightly with the egg mixture and sprinkle with sugar. Repeat with remaining dough.

8. Bake at 360 °F for 15–20 minutes.

Carla pauses in her pie-making for a hug from Paula Abdul.

PEACH COBBLER

SERVES 8 | **Skill Level: MODERATE** | **Cook Time: 45 mins.** | **Prep Time: 20 mins.** | **Cost: $**

I couldn't love anything more than a ripe peach, the kind that is so juicy you need to eat it standing over the sink. My Grandma Thelma's peach cobblers were the dessert highlight of the summer. She would make it with a crust on the bottom that was crumbly and flaky on the outside, and soft, smooth, and juicy on the inside, like a dumpling. My version backs off a bit from Grandma's use of sugar, but I do that with a lot of desserts. You need to remember to balance with salt. That makes all the flavors bloom.

FOR THE FILLING:

2 tablespoons butter

4 cups peaches, peeled and sliced

½ cup sugar, plus more to sprinkle

½ cup brown sugar

½ teaspoon cinnamon

¼ teaspoon nutmeg

¼ cup water

¼ cup amaretto

FOR THE CRUST:

2 cups all-purpose flour

½ cup sugar

4 teaspoons baking powder

1 teaspoon salt

2 tablespoons shortening

4 tablespoons butter, divided

½ cup yogurt

⅓ cup milk, plus more to brush

1 tablespoon water

1. Preheat the oven to 350 °F.

2. Heat the butter in a large cast-iron skillet over medium-high heat until it foams and subsides. Add the peaches, sugars, cinnamon, nutmeg, water, and amaretto. Cook until broken down slightly, about 10–15 minutes.

3. In a bowl or food processor, combine the flour, sugar, baking powder, and salt. Cut in the shortening with your fingertips or in the food processor (using quick pulses), then cut the butter into the dry mixture using the same method.

4. Combine the yogurt, milk, and water. Make a well in the dry ingredients, and pour the wet mixture in. Using a wooden spoon or rubber spatula, stir until just combined and pour into a 9 x 9 baking dish.

5. Drop tablespoonfuls on top of the peach mixture. Brush the exposed dough with milk, and then sprinkle sugar over the whole thing. Transfer to the oven and bake for 20–30 minutes, until the crust is golden brown.

ZOMBIE

SERVES 1 | **Skill Level: EASY** | **Prep Time: 10 mins.** | **Cost: $**

What party would be complete without a rum cocktail? Not one that Clinton Kelly would throw. And, if television and the movies are to be believed, there are sure to be a few vampires and zombies whenever people gather these days, and you want to stay on their good side. So here is the Zombie cocktail. Daphne asked me, "Is the point of this to kill the zombie or wake it back up?" That depends on how healthy your zombie friends are. They go down easy, so be careful or you will wake up feeling like a zombie the next morning.

1 teaspoon Falernum
1 ounce lime juice
1 ounce orange juice
1 ounce pineapple juice
1 ounce orange curaçao
1 ounce dark rum
2 ounces gold rum
Ice
1 slice orange
1 wedge pineapple
1 Maraschino cherry
1 sprig mint

1. Put the Falernum, lime juice, orange juice, pineapple juice, curaçao, dark rum, and gold rum into a mixing glass over several ice cubes and stir well. Pour over cracked ice in a 14-ounce Collins glass.

2. Garnish with a slice of orange, a wedge of pineapple, a cherry, and a sprig of mint.

The word is falernum

Falernum sounds like the name of a villain who has a walk-on part on *Game of Thrones*, but actually it's a delicious mix of almond, ginger, clove, lime, and vanilla. It is absolutely wonderful in cocktails. I suspect it also wouldn't be too bad in gingerbread batter, or a fish stew. If serving to a vampire, beware: it may put them in a romantic mood, and that can sting.

WHITE SANGRIA

SERVES 6 | Skill Level: EASY | Cook Time: 5 mins. | Prep Time: 15 mins. | Cost: $

Inactive Prep Time: 12 hrs.

Our White Sangria is a great summer drink because it allows you to feel lighter than a big, chewy red wine sangria … or, in a word, more summery. It pairs really easily with a lot of summer foods. If you're barbecuing chicken, White Sangria goes really nice. Imagine getting some fresh fish that you just caught and putting them on the grill, then washing it down with this sangria. It's summer in a glass. Heaven!

1 cup water

1 cup sugar

2 bottles crisp white wine

2 apricots, sliced

2 white peaches, sliced

1 lemon, sliced

1 quart sparkling water

½ cup mint leaves

1 cup frozen white grapes

1. To make a simple syrup, combine the water and sugar in a saucepan, and heat just until the sugar has dissolved, about 5 minutes, then set aside to cool.

2. Place the wine in a large pitcher or punch bowl, and add the apricots, peaches, lemon, and ½–1 cup of the simple syrup, depending on how sweet you like it. Refrigerate overnight.

3. Remove from the fridge and top with the sparkling water, and stir in the mint and frozen grapes.

SUMMER

211

FROZEN FRUIT SORBET

SERVES 6 | **Skill Level: EASY** | **Prep Time: 5 mins.** | **Inactive Prep time: 2 hrs.** | **Cost: $**

One of the joys of summer is sweet, juicy ripe fruit. I agree with Carla, who said you can't do better than peaches, picked at the peak of flavor and tossed in the blender. Canned fruit, packed in sugary syrup, just doesn't cut it, health-wise or taste-wise. This is a dessert that's sweet but won't make your fillings vibrate. You simply put all the ingredients in a blender, freeze, and serve. If Michael doesn't mind my poaching on his turf, I'd like to add this to our 5-in-5 recipes. Actually, it's 3 ingredients in about 3 minutes!

3 cups frozen peaches

1⅓ cups coconut milk or almond milk, plus more if needed

2 tablespoons honey

1. Using a blender, combine all ingredients until smooth. Pour into freezer-safe container. Freeze for 2 hours, scoop, and serve.

213

Q&A
WITH

Carla

Q. **You didn't start out as a cook. You were a model. What got you into cooking?**

Carla: Before I became a chef, I worked as a fashion model in France and I never cooked. I wasn't interested in what happens between the grocery store and food getting to the table. My girlfriends would always be in the kitchen, cooking and talking about how their mothers would make things. I had nothing to contribute. But I grew interested. That sort of comes with the territory when you live in France, so I started buying cookbooks and I was fascinated by them.

Q: **What kind of cookbooks?**

Carla: When I lived in France and then London, I would look for books on a subject instead of a particular author or chef. It would be about bread or it would be on breakfast (because my friends and I were doing lots of brunches then).

Carla and Paula Deen—two smiling Southern gals!

Q: **You have little folk sayings and made-up words. What's with that?**

Carla: I do ticky-boo, doink, slap my momma, and, of course, hootie-hoo, which just came out one day when I was on *Top Chef*. I don't know where these things come from, because I don't think about them until I'm saying them. They just occur to me when I am cooking and talking to people, especially when I am teaching. They are made-up words that people somehow connect with. They add some emotion to what could be a rote cooking lesson.

Q: **How do you like being the go-go dancer on the show? How did that happen?**

Carla: Kind of a fluke. One day, I was watching Mario and Michael and marveled at how they could cook, and talk, and look at the camera all at the same time and make it look so easy. Things didn't come that naturally to me. I felt like I wasn't really focusing on my food the way I wanted. And when you don't focus, you can't communicate. So one day they were playing some really good music when we went to a break, and I just went up and I started dancing. The audience really liked it, and it made me feel free in spirit. When we came back from break, I was more relaxed. Everyone complimented me on that particular segment, and I said, "Oh, that's because I went and burned my energy on the music." So Gordon Elliott (our executive producer) looked at me for a second and said, "Carla, from now on you will have music every time you do a segment. Give us your playlist." Now I get to go up to dance with every chance. It really connects me to the audience and to my cooking.

Q: **It's spontaneous, like your cooking. People like the spontaneity of the show.**

Carla: I'm a performer—I consider myself a MacGyver in the kitchen, so if something goes wrong, it's all about the recovery. That's the way it was for me in real life before TV. For many years, it was just me and my catering business. I didn't have money to trash something and then get more ingredients, so I had to make it work. It's the same on the show. It's real. Things don't always come out perfectly. One time we had a cheesecake that had a big crack in it, and we tried to cover it over with some chocolate we were working with. We added some oil to the chocolate in an attempt to get it all melted and smooth again, but that didn't work. Something just kicked in and told me to try rolling the chocolate between plastic wrap and then spread it all over the cake. It worked! I sometimes tell people if you're on a desert island or if you're having an emergency, you want me on your team, because I'm the person who can probably get out of it. I'm not going to panic. I'm all about "We can do this."

Q: **In one sentence, what is your philosophy on cooking?**

Carla: It sounds kind of mystical, but I think what this does is give power back to people to learn and then to trust their own cooking instincts. You have to start with a sense that it's an honor to cook for people, you need to take it very seriously. Have fun, but take it seriously.

Q: **That's three sentences.**

Carla: I don't always have to follow the recipe.

What Not to Bring to a Party

YOU FINALLY SCORE THAT INVITATION to the best dinner party in town and you're wondering what kind of gift you should bring. Well, I'll tell you what not to bring so that you are the season's most requested guest. Oh, somebody's at the door! Let's see who it is!

Daphne: Hi, Clinton!

Clinton: Hi, Daphne!

Daphne: I brought you some flowers!

Clinton: Oh, thanks.

Clinton I cannot believe Daphne bought me these tacky flowers. Now I have to trim the stems and find a vase and put them in water.

Now here's the deal about bringing flowers to somebody who's hosting a party. It's really inconvenient for a host to cut the stems, get rid of the paper, find a vase, and put 'em in water. So don't do it. Okay? What you can do is the day before somebody's having a party, have flowers delivered to them. And that way, they can incorporate them into their design scheme. Or, even better, to thank them for spending their whole day entertaining you, you can send flowers the next day, so that they can enjoy them in the privacy of their own home.

Clinton: Somebody else is here! I feel like Pee-wee Herman a little bit. Okay. Who is it? Oh! It's Carla!

Carla: Clinton, I brought you a seven-layer dip. Let me just tell you. It's Michael Symon's sister's recipe!

Clinton: Great!

Clinton Hellooo. I made my world-famous six-layer dip. Is Carla trying to show me up with seven layers? Don't bring unwanted food. That can really throw off a host's game. If they ask for it, then that's great—bring it. But if they didn't ask for it, don't bring food. What you can do is bring a box of chocolates and tell the host that they are to enjoy a little bit later on or maybe even for dessert. Another nice thing to do is to bring a plate of scones that the host can eat the next morning, because he or she will have been spending the whole day cooking and will appreciate a homemade gift for breakfast

Clinton: More people! Love it! It's Michael Symon!

Michael: Clinton! As a good Greek boy, I bring you a sculpture for your table! It was either that or plastic for furniture. I stole it from my mom.

Clinton Gee whiz! I thought Michael and I were friends. Does he really think I have no taste? Do not bring a decorative object to somebody's house. And especially do not expect them to display it. Okay? But what you can do is bring a nice seasonal plate or platter, or, if it's a holiday party, a holiday decoration is a nice option because your host can display it during the holidays and then put it in a closet for eleven months of the year.

Mario: Ciao, Clinton!

Clinton: Oh, Mario!

Mario: I brought you a killer bottle of Barolo. Let's crack it open right now.

Clinton But I already picked out the perfect sauvignon blanc and Pinot Noir. This Barolo does no-go-lo.
Here's the thing about bringing wine. Wine is a wonderful gift. However, you should not expect it to be drunk that day or at that event, because your host probably spent time picking out wine already. So when you present it to your host, you can suggest that it is not for the party but to enjoy later in the evening or for their wine cellar.

Mario: Oh, I also forgot to tell you, my cousin Quintillio just got out of Rahway Prison!

Clinton Please say you're kidding!
Never bring an uninvited guest! Really bad form, plus if it's his first meal since getting out of prison, he may eat everything in sight.
Follow these tips and you'll be the perfect guest for your next party.

Carla and RuPaul bust a move!

Our Last Supper

IT'S A TIME-HONORED FANTASY GAME: If you had to pick one last meal, what would it be? You kind of wish it were a Top Ten list, but they asked for just one.

Michael: **BEET AND GOAT CHEESE RAVIOLI WITH BUTTER AND FRESH TARRAGON**

I would have Bobby Flay make me a burger—because if I'm going out, I'm going out big. Paul Kahan would roast me an entire suckling pig—he owns a great restaurant called Blackbird in Chicago—and I would have a little bit of Marc Vetri's raviolis and a perfectly roasted chicken from Jonathan Waxman from Barbuto. Lizzie, in front of the fireplace at home.

SOUNDTRACK: Led Zeppelin, Van Halen, Stevie Ray Vaughan—let it rip!

Carla:

HAMBURGER AND ONION RINGS AND GINGER LEMONADE

My grandfather, George Hall Sr., had a five-and-dime store, where he ran numbers in the back. Up front we had nickel candy, big burgers, and the world's best onion rings. I think onion rings are really special—more special than French fries. And to drink, I just want to say that my ginger lemonade is the nectar of the gods.

SOUNDTRACK: Anything I can really dance to.

Clinton:

LOBSTER THERMIDOR

The main event would be lobster thermidor. I first tasted it when I was thirteen at the Clam Box in Carmel, California, and I was like, "This is the food of the gods." Ever since, I have it about once a year on a special occasion. It's a little on the expensive side . . . but it's your last meal, so charge it—you're never going to get the bill.

SOUNDTRACK: Sondheim all the way, probably the soundtrack to *Company*.

Daphne:

CHICKPEA AND DUMPLING STEW

I'm sitting in a French bistro, there are candles around me. I've already finished a bottle of Verdejo, and I am now sitting down to my green salad . . . then a huge, perfect baguette slathered with salted honey butter . . . then I'm going to eat my vegetarian version of chicken and dumplings that I make with chickpea soup. When I discovered matzo ball soup, I wanted to be Jewish; when I discovered chicken and dumplings, I wanted to be from the South. Today, I just want to be me.

SOUNDTRACK: I've got Christmas carols going all the dinner, then David Guetta when I open that second bottle of Super Tuscan.

Mario:

TRUFFLE OMELET

Piedmont, in truffle season, surrounded by the great vines of Barolo and Nebbiolo—delicious, evocative, powerful, and simple. The egg is perhaps the single most perfect food, as it encapsulates both our wonder with which came first and the idea of creation. It's amazing what an egg represents! Food is a little bit about philosophy, a little bit about technique, a lot about lighting. I'm making a simple omelet. The truffles are expensive, about $3,500, and put it on Clinton's credit card.

SOUNDTRACK: R.E.M., U2, and Jimi Hendrix.

Acknowledgments

Mark Schneider, who makes sure that every step this show takes is perfectly planned and executed. Without his meticulous eye for detail, the show would have no lights, no cameras, and no ovens.

Aimee Rosen Householder, our midwife/producer with extraordinary creative instincts, who cheerily provides midnight rewrites and big, bold ideas. Without you nothing would be in the ovens.

Pat De Fazio, you cut and pasted the emerging face of the show, frame by frame, and set us on a glide path to Victual Valhalla. You have the skill and speed of a caffeinated ninja.

Paul Starke, you were born to produce this show (or be the world's leading sit-down comic). You show us every day how far you can push a plate of pasta into an hour of broadcasting fun.

Randy Barone, you're a gift from ABC to the show, a vice president who "got it" from the start and a full creative partner in birthing the biggest TV food program in the world. It's a kick to do it with you every day.

Brian Frons, we owe you a huge personal debt. You believed in us personally and professionally from day one. It was your wise, experienced voice that steadied our rudder during those early days of confusion.

Anne Sweeney. Because every project needs someone with the courage to throw the big switch. No one had ever done this kind of show, but you understood it immediately. Without your support and belief, there would never have been a *Chew*. It was your vision of bringing people back to the family table that made this show a reality.

Sophie Elliott, who has listened lovingly to hundreds of hours of bad ideas over the years and provided insight and support to create the good ones—like *The Chew*. X.

The Chew list of recipes

FALL

Roasted Autumn Vegetables, 15

Chestnut Crepes with Mushrooms and Radicchio Salad, 16

Eggs with Sweet Potato Apple Pancakes, 18

Monte Cristo Sandwich, 20

Chile Chicken Flautas, 21

Eggplant Parmigianino, 24

Stuffed Mushrooms, 25

Spaghetti Squash Fritters, 27

Wine-Stained Pasta with Sausage Meatballs and Cauliflower, 29

General Tso's Chicken, 31

Roasted Chicken with Sweet Potatoes and Sage, 32

Cast-Iron Pork Pie, 34

Crispy Lime and Cilantro Chicken Wings, 37

Lemon Sage Turkey, 42

Chestnut Merguez Stuffing, 44

Mushroom and Vegetable Stuffing, 45

Pan-Seared Turkey with Gremolata, 47

Brussels Sprouts à la "Russ" with Walnuts and Capers, 48

Chocolate Pumpkin Pie, 51

Batter Fried Apple Rings, 52

Chew Chew Clusters, 53

Ten-Gallon Apple Pie, 54

BLT Bloody Mary, 56

The Stinton, 59

Pomegranate Sunset, 61

Cranberry Soda, 62

WINTER

Warrior Salad, 70

Winter Green Salad with Pears, Aged Cheddar, and Almonds, 71

Braised Pork Shanks, 72

White Beans, Pork, and Collard Greens Soup, 74

Chilaquiles, 79

Eggs in Hell, 80

Eggs in Heaven, 82

Slow Cooker Peachy Chicken, 83

Grilled Chicken and Fennel Salad, 84

Pork au Poivre, 87

Champagne Crown Roast, 89

Holiday Mac 'n' Cheese Casserole, 90

Michael's Chicken Chili, 94

Mario's Restrictor Plate Chili, 95

Chili con Carla, 97

Daphne's Veggie Chili, 99

Deep-Dish Pizza Casserole, 100

Meatloaf alla Mario, 103

Chocaholic Whoopie Pies, 105

Grilled Bacon, Chocolate-Hazelnut Sandwich, 108

Hot Muttered Bum, 112

Roles Royce, 113

Potato Leek Soup, 114

Irish Soda Bread, 116

Super Bowl Punch, 118

The Warm and Toasty, 119

Spicy Grapefruit Margarita, aka "The Clinton Caliente," 120

SPRING

Spicy Shrimp Cocktail, 128

Ricotta, Mint, and Spring Pea Bruschetta, 129

Carrots with Feta and Mint, 130

Spring Vegetable Pasta with
    Chive Bread Crumbs, 133

Bacon, Egg, and Cheese Casserole, 134

Asparagus and Goat Cheese Frittata, 136

Roman-Style Artichokes, 137

Grilled Salmon with Shaved Carrots
    and Peanut Salad, 138

Beer-Battered Fish and Chips, 140

Mom's Chicken with Saffron,
    Olives, and Onions, 142

Big Turkey Meatball Subs, 143

Paella, 146

Curried Chicken and Dumplings, 148

Greek Easter Leg of Lamb, 149

Pot Roast with Shaved Carrot Salad, 152

Bahn Mi, 153

Red Velvet Cake, 154

Sebadas, 156

Sweet Phyllo Packets, 157

Coconut Pecan Pound Cake, 159

Banana Puddin, 160

Mint Julep, 162

Strawberry White Wine Cooler Punch, 163

Rhubarb Punch, 164

SUMMER

Watermelon Gazpacho, 172

White Gazpacho with Frozen Grapes, 174

Grilled Vegetable and
    Peach Summer Salad, 175

Sweet Corn with Onions and Basil, 176

Summer Scafata, 177

Grilled Eggplant with Greek Yogurt, 179

Daphne's Superfoods Smoothie, 180

Mussels alla Piastra, 181

Fried Clam Sandwich, 182

Michael Symon's Twice-Fried Chicken, 185

Grandma Thelma's Fried Chicken, 186

Fettuccine with Lobster, Tomatoes,
    and Saffron, 187

Corn Doggin', 188

Big Mike Burger, 189

Cheese-Stuffed Mortadella on Bruschetta, 195

Turkey Sliders, 196

Daphne's Best Burger, 198

Dry Rub Baby Back Ribs with
    Scalloped Potatoes, 200

T-Bone Fiorentina, 202

Blueberry Hand Pies, 204

Peach Cobbler, 207

Zombie, 208

White Sangria, 211

Frozen Fruit Sorbet, 212

Index

Agave, 157
Almonds:
   White Gazpacho with
      Frozen Grapes, 174
   Winter Green Salad with
      Pears, Aged Cheddar and,
      71
Anchovies, 85
   Grilled Chicken and Fennel
      Salad, 84–85
Apple(s):
   Cider Syrup, 52
   Pie, Ten-Gallon, 54–55
   Pork au Poivre, 87
   Rings, Batter Fried, 52
   Sweet Potato Pancakes,
      Eggs with, 18
   tasting, 54
Artichokes, Roman-Style, 137
Asparagus:
   and Goat Cheese Frittata,
      136
   Grilled Vegetable and Peach
      Summer Salad, 175
   Spring Vegetable Pasta with
      Chive Bread Crumbs, 133

Bacon:
   Chocolate-Hazelnut
      Sandwich, Grilled, 108
   Egg, and Cheese Casserole,
      134–35
   Holiday Mac 'n' Cheese
      Casserole, 90–91
Bahn Mi, 153

Banana(s):
   Grilled Bacon, Chocolate-
      Hazelnut Sandwich, 108
   Puddin, 160
Basil:
   Grilled Vegetable and Peach
      Summer Salad, 175
   Sweet Corn with Onions
      and, 176
Beans:
   Daphne's Veggie Chili, 99
   fava, 132
   Mario's Restrictor Plate
      Chili, 95
   Michael's Chicken Chili, 94
   soaking, 75
   Spring Vegetable Pasta with
      Chive Bread Crumbs, 133
   White, Pork and Collard
      Greens Soup, 74
Beef:
   Bahn Mi, 153
   Big Mike Burger, 189–90
   Chili con Carla, 97
   Mario's Restrictor Plate
      Chili, 95
   Meatloaf alla Mario, 103–4
   Pot Roast with Shaved
      Carrot Salad, 152
   T-Bone Fiorentina, 202
Beverages:
   BLT Bloody Mary, 56
   Cranberry Soda, 62
   Hot Muttered Bum, 112
   Mint Julep, 162

   Pomegranate Sunset, 61
   Rhubarb Punch, 164
   Roles Royce, 113
   Spicy Grapefruit Margarita,
      aka "The Clinton
      Caliente," 120
   The Stinton, 59
   Strawberry White Wine
      Cooler Punch, 163
   Super Bowl Punch, 118
   The Warm and Toasty, 119
   White Sangria, 211
   Zombie, 208
Blueberry Hand Pies, 204–5
Bread, Irish Soda, 116
Bruschetta:
   Cheese-Stuffed Mortadella
      on, 195
   Ricotta, Mint, and Spring
      Pea, 129
Brussels Sprouts:
   Roasted Autumn
      Vegetables, 15
   à la "Russ" with Walnuts
      and Capers, 48

Cakes:
   Coconut Pecan Pound, 159
   Red Velvet, 154–55
Capers, Brussels Sprouts à
      la "Russ" with Walnuts
      and, 48
Caramel:
   Chew Chew Clusters, 53
   Sauce, 53

Carrot(s):
  with Feta and Mint, 130
  Meatloaf alla Mario, 103–4
  Roasted Autumn
    Vegetables, 15
  Shaved, and Peanut Salad,
    Grilled Salmon with, 138
  Shaved, Salad, Pot Roast
    with, 152
Cauliflower, Wine-Stained
  Pasta with Sausage
  Meatballs and, 29–30
Cheese:
  Bacon, and Egg Casserole,
    134–35
  Big Turkey Meatball Subs,
    143
  Carrots with Feta and Mint,
    130
  Cast-Iron Pork Pie, 34
  Chilaquiles, 79
  Chile Chicken Flautas, 21–23
  Deep-Dish Pizza Casserole,
    100–102
  Eggplant Parmigianino, 24
  Goat, and Asparagus
    Frittata, 136
  Macaroni and, Holiday
    Casserole, 90–91
  Meatloaf alla Mario, 103–4
  Monte Cristo Sandwich, 20
  Ricotta, Mint, and Spring
    Pea Bruschetta, 129
  Sebadas, 156
  -Stuffed Mortadella on
    Bruschetta, 195
  Sweet Phyllo Packets, 157
  Winter Green Salad with
    Pears, Aged Cheddar, and
    Almonds, 71
Chestnut:
  Crepes with Mushrooms
    and Radicchio Salad,
    16–17

Merguez Stuffing, 44
Chicken:
  Chile Flautas, 21–23
  Chili, Michael's, 94
  and Dumplings, Curried, 148
  General Tso's, 31
  Grandma Thelma's Fried,
    186
  Grilled, and Fennel Salad,
    84–85
  Michael Symon's Twice-
    Fried, 185
  Roasted, with Sweet
    Potatoes and Sage, 32
  with Saffron, Olives, and
    Onions, 142
  Slow Cooker Peachy, 83
  Wings, Crispy Lime and
    Cilantro, 37
Chickpeas:
  Curried Chicken and
    Dumplings, 148
  Warrior Salad, 70
Chilaquiles, 79
Chile(s), 21
  Chicken Flautas, 21–23
Chili:
  con Carla, 97
  Daphne's Veggie, 99
  Mario's Restrictor Plate, 95
  Michael's Chicken, 94
Chive:
  Bacon, Egg, and Cheese
    Casserole, 134–35
  Bread Crumbs, Spring
    Vegetable Pasta with, 133
Chocolate:
  Chew Chew Clusters, 53
  Chocaholic Whoopie Pies,
    105–7
  -Hazelnut Bacon Sandwich,
    Grilled, 108
  Pumpkin Pie, 51
  Red Velvet Cake, 154–55

Cilantro and Lime Chicken
  Wings, Crispy, 37
Clam(s):
  Fried, Sandwich, 182
  Paella, 146
Coconut milk, 148
  Curried Chicken and
    Dumplings, 148
  Frozen Fruit Sorbet, 212
Coconut Pecan Pound Cake,
  159
Collard greens, 74
  White Beans, and Pork
    Soup, 74
Corn:
  Daphne's Veggie Chili, 99
  Grilled Vegetable and Peach
    Summer Salad, 175
  Sweet, with Onions and
    Basil, 176
Corn Doggin', 188
Crepes:
  Chestnut, with Mushrooms
    and Radicchio Salad,
    16–17
  making in advance, 17
Cucumbers:
  Grilled Vegetable and Peach
    Summer Salad, 175
  Watermelon Gazpacho, 172

Desserts:
  Banana Puddin, 160
  Batter Fried Apple Rings, 52
  Blueberry Hand Pies, 204–5
  Chew Chew Clusters, 53
  Chocaholic Whoopie Pies,
    105–7
  Chocolate Pumpkin Pie, 51
  Coconut Pecan Pound Cake,
    159
  Frozen Fruit Sorbet, 212
  Grilled Bacon, Chocolate-
    Hazelnut Sandwich, 108

Peach Cobbler, 207
Red Velvet Cake, 154–55
Sebadas, 156
Sweet Phyllo Packets, 157
Ten-Gallon Apple Pie, 54–55
Dumplings, Curried Chicken
  and, 148

Egg(s):
  Asparagus and Goat Cheese
    Frittata, 136
  Bacon, and Cheese
    Casserole, 134–35
  Chilaquiles, 79
  in Heaven, 82
  in Hell, 80
  Mario's Restrictor Plate
    Chili, 95
  Monte Cristo Sandwich, 20
  scrambled, 78
  with Sweet Potato Apple
    Pancakes, 18
Eggplant:
  Cast-Iron Pie, 34
  Grilled, with Greek Yogurt,
    179
  Parmigianino, 24
  roasting, 179
  salting, 24

Fennel:
  Salad, Grilled Chicken and,
    84–85
  Summer Scafata, 177
Fish. See Seafood
Frittata, Asparagus and Goat
  Cheese, 136
Fritters, Spaghetti Squash, 27
Frying foods, 36

Garlic:
  Lemon Sage Turkey, 42–43
  Tarragon Aioli, 199
Gazpacho:

Watermelon, 172
White, with Frozen Grapes,
  174
Grapes, Frozen, White
  Gazpacho with, 174
Gremolata, Pan-Seared Turkey
  with, 47
Griddles, 181
Grits, 82
  Eggs in Heaven, 82

Hazelnut-Chocolate, Bacon
  Sandwich, Grilled, 108

Lamb:
  Greek Easter Leg of, 149–50
  grilling, 150
Leek(s), 114
  Potato Soup, 114
Lemon Sage Turkey, 42–43
Lentils, 15
  Roasted Autumn
    Vegetables, 15
Lime and Cilantro Chicken
  Wings, Crispy, 37
Lobster, Fettuccine with
  Tomatoes, Saffron and,
  187

Mac 'n' Cheese Casserole,
  Holiday, 90–91
Mandolin, 139
Marinades, 84
Meat:
  browning, 153
  Cheese-Stuffed Mortadella
    on Bruschetta, 195
  Greek Easter Leg of Lamb,
    149–50
  grilling lamb, 150
  See also Bacon; Beef; Pork;
    Sausage
Meatball(s):
  Sausage, Wine-Stained

Pasta with Cauliflower
  and, 29–30
  Subs, Big Turkey, 143
Meatloaf alla Mario, 103–4
Mint:
  Carrots with Feta and, 130
  Ricotta, and Spring Pea
    Bruschetta, 129
Mortadella, Cheese-Stuffed, on
  Bruschetta, 195
Mushroom(s):
  Cast-Iron Pie, 34
  Chestnut Crepes with
    Radicchio Salad and,
    16–17
  Daphne's Best Burger, 198–
    99
  Stuffed, 25
  and Vegetable Stuffing, 45
Mussels:
  Paella, 146
  alla Piastra, 181

Olives, Mom's Chicken with
  Saffron, Onions and, 142
Onions:
  Mom's Chicken with
    Saffron, Olives and, 142
  Pickled Red, 190
  Sweet Corn with Basil and,
    176

Paella, 146
Pancakes, Sweet Potato Apple,
  Eggs with, 18
Pasta, 90, 132
  Fettuccine with Lobster,
    Tomatoes, and Saffron,
    187
  Holiday Mac 'n' Cheese
    Casserole, 90–91
  Spring Vegetable, with
    Chive Bread Crumbs,
    133

Pasta (continued)
  Wine-Stained, with
    Sausage Meatballs and
    Cauliflower, 29–30
Pea(s):
  Paella, 146
  Spring, Ricotta and Mint
    Bruschetta, 129
  Spring Vegetable Pasta with
    Chive Bread Crumbs, 133
Peach(es):
  Cobbler, 207
  Frozen Fruit Sorbet, 212
  Slow Cooker Chicken, 83
  and Vegetable Summer
    Salad, Grilled, 175
Peanut(s):
  Chew Chew Clusters, 53
  and Shaved Carrots Salad,
    Grilled Salmon with, 138
Pears, Winter Green Salad
  with Aged Cheddar,
  Almonds and, 71
Pecan Coconut Pound Cake,
  159
Phyllo Packets, Sweet, 157
Pies:
  Chocolate Pumpkin, 51
  Ten-Gallon Apple, 54–55
Pizza Casserole, Deep-Dish,
  100–102
Pork:
  Champagne Crown Roast,
    89
  Dry Rub Baby Back Ribs
    with Scalloped Potatoes,
    200–201
  Pie, Cast-Iron, 34
  au Poivre, 87
  Shanks, Braised, 72–73
  White Beans, and Collard
    Greens Soup, 74
Potato(es):
  Cast-Iron Pork Pie, 34

Greek Easter Leg of Lamb,
  149–50
Leek Soup, 114
Scalloped, Dry Rub Baby
  Back Ribs with, 200–201
Poultry. See Chicken; Turkey
Pumpkin:
  Chocolate Pie, 51
  Holiday Mac 'n' Cheese
    Casserole, 90–91

Quinoa, 70
  Warrior Salad, 70

Radicchio Salad, Chestnut
  Crepes with Mushrooms
  and, 16–17
Rice:
  General Tso's Chicken, 31
  Paella, 146
Rosemary:
  Lemon Sage Turkey, 42–43
  T-Bone Fiorentina, 202

Saffron, 147
  Fettuccine with Lobster,
    Tomatoes and, 187
  Mom's Chicken with Olives,
    Onions and, 142
  Paella, 146
Sage, 27
  Lemon Turkey, 42–43
  Roasted Chicken with Sweet
    Potatoes and, 32
  Spaghetti Squash Fritters, 27
Salad:
  Fennel, Grilled Chicken and,
    84–85
  Grilled Vegetable and Peach
    Summer, 175
  Radicchio, Chestnut Crepes
    with Mushrooms and,
    16–17
  Warrior, 70

Winter Green, with Pears,
  Aged Cheddar, and
  Almonds, 71
Salmon, Grilled, with Shaved
  Carrots and Peanut Salad,
  138
Sandwiches:
  Bahn Mi, 153
  Big Mike Burger, 189–90
  Big Turkey Meatball Subs,
    143
  Daphne's Best Burger, 198–
    99
  Fried Clam, 182
  Grilled Bacon, Chocolate-
    Hazelnut, 108
  Monte Christo, 20
  Turkey Sliders, 196
Sausage:
  Chestnut Merguez Stuffing,
    44
  Meatballs, Wine-Stained
    Pasta with Cauliflower
    and, 29–30
  Meatloaf alla Mario, 103–4
  Paella, 146
Scafata, Summer, 177
Seafood:
  Beer-Battered Fish and
    Chips, 140
  Corn Doggin', 188
  Fettuccine with Lobster,
    Tomatoes, and Saffron,
    187
  Fried Clam Sandwich, 182
  Grilled Salmon with Shaved
    Carrots and Peanut Salad,
    138
  grilling fish, 138
  Mussels alla Piastra, 181
  Paella, 146
  Spicy Shrimp Cocktail, 128
Sebadas, 156
Shrimp:

Cocktail, Spicy, 128
Corn Doggin', 188
Paella, 146
Skillets, 80
Slow cookers, 83
Smoothie, Daphne's
    Superfoods, 180
Sorbet, Frozen Fruit, 212
Soups:
    Potato Leek, 114
    Watermelon Gazpacho, 172
    White Beans, Pork, and
        Collard Greens, 74
    White Gazpacho with
        Frozen Grapes, 174
Spices, roasting, 138
Spinach:
    Meatloaf alla Mario, 103–4
    Slow Cooker Peachy
        Chicken, 83
Squash:
    Cast-Iron Pie, 34
    Holiday Mac 'n' Cheese
        Casserole, 90–91
    Roasted Autumn
        Vegetables, 15
    Spaghetti, Fritters, 27
Stuffing:
    Chestnut Merguez, 44
    Mushroom and Vegetable, 45
Sweet Potato(es):
    Apple Pancakes, Eggs with,
        18
    Roasted Chicken with Sage
        and, 32

Tapenade, 85
    Grilled Chicken and Fennel
        Salad, 84–85
Tomato(es), 187
    Big Turkey Meatball Subs,
        143
    Chili con Carla, 97
    Daphne's Veggie Chili, 99
    Deep-Dish Pizza Casserole,
        100–102
    Eggplant Parmigianino, 24
    Eggs in Hell, 80
    Fettuccine with Lobster,
        Saffron and, 187
    Grilled Vegetable and Peach
        Summer Salad, 175
    Mario's Restrictor Plate
        Chili, 95
    Michael's Chicken Chili, 94
    Paella, 146
    Sauce, Mario's Basic, 30
    Summer Scafata, 177
    Watermelon Gazpacho, 172
    Wine-Stained Pasta with
        Sausage Meatballs and
        Cauliflower, 29–30
Tortillas:
    Chilaquiles, 79
    Chile Chicken Flautas, 21–23
    Mario's Restrictor Plate
        Chili, 95
Turkey:
    Lemon Sage, 42–43
    Meatball Subs, Big, 143
    Monte Cristo Sandwich, 20

    Pan-Seared, with Gremolata,
        47
    Sliders, 196

Vegetable(s):
    and Mushroom Stuffing,
        45
    and Peach Summer Salad,
        Grilled, 175
    Roasted Autumn, 15
    sautéing, 133
    Spring, Pasta with Chive
        Bread Crumbs, 133

Walnuts, Brussels Sprouts à
    la "Russ" with Capers
    and, 48
Watermelon Gazpacho, 172
Whoopie Pies, Chocaholic,
    105–7

Yogurt:
    Greek, Grilled Eggplant
        with, 179
    Tzatziki Sauce, 150

Zucchini:
    Corn Doggin', 188
    Daphne's Veggie Chili,
        99
    Grilled Vegetable and
        Peach Summer Salad, 175
    Summer Scafata, 177